TREVOR BARNES

TERRY WAITE

MAN WITH A MISSION

WILLIAM B. EERDMANS PUBLISHING COMPANY
GRAND RAPIDS, MICHIGAN

ISBN 0-8028-0332-6

CONTENTS

LIST OF ILLUSTRATIONS

INTRODUCTION

With discreet and poignant understatement worthy of the Archbishop of Canterbury's Special Envoy himself, the nameboard in the porter's lodge at Lambeth Palace tells a solemn story in shorthand. The staff who are inside at work in the Palace have slid their wooden panels across the wooden slot to disclose the word "IN". Terry Waite, at the time of writing missing for two months, presumed kidnapped, is "OUT".

"Mindful that prayer is the first resort, not the last," said the Archbishop, "we offer prayers for peace and justice in Lebanon, the release of all hostages held in that country, and the speedy return of Terry Waite from his humanitarian mission." Dr Robert Runcie's words to the General Synod of the Church of England in February 1987 were spoken on behalf of members of the Anglican Church worldwide but their appeal travelled far wider, reaching men and women of goodwill everywhere who have seen in Terry Waite a simple, attractive, and honest man doing his best, against all the odds, to bring a grain more understanding into the world.

Through this unassuming envoy, whose face has become instantly recognizable to everyone – those who have lost contact with the Church are suddenly reminded of its presence, those who have lost hope in it are encouraged, and those who have lost interest in it do for once take notice.

Here is that rare and powerful combination – goodness

and strength coupled with humanity that does not seem out of reach. At home as much with the man in the street as with the bishops and archbishops of the world, Terry Waite has become a unique phenomenon in the Church. Not that he is without his detractors, who accuse him of being a foolish innocent meddling in an adult's world. They will point to the fact that for every one hostage Mr Waite has rescued another half dozen or so remain captive. But how can success be measured? And would those freed from Middle Eastern jails use the same standard as those who sit back comfortably at home and criticize?

It is true that question marks hang over this latest mission to the Lebanon, raising doubts of which Terry Waite himself was fully aware. His decision to return to honour the pledges he made to individual men taken hostage was done in the full knowledge of the risk. Often he has said that when he leaves on one of his missions he leaves behind him the family of a potential hostage. And still he takes the risk. Why?

The following pages suggest an answer. It is only partial and we hope that Mr Waite himself will soon be able to add more detail to this interim profile. But what emerges even here is a lifetime spent in service to his Christian faith and a vocation which has steadily, irresistibly been fashioned at every twist and turn of his fascinating and unpredictable life.

1

THE MAN AND THE MISSION

The least remarkable thing about Terry Waite is his height. It is, of course, the first thing which comes to mind when describing him, and invariably the first thing to which those who have had particular reason to be grateful for his help refer. It contributes to "the reassuring figure" – half Russian Orthodox patriarch, half Rugby League full-back – which put at rest the minds of single missionary workers living alone on Namirembe Hill when he did his unofficial rounds of the mission houses in Kampala during the lawless days of Amin's Uganda. It adds to the image of "the jovial giant who always filled people with confidence" when he travelled round the world in the seventies, helping Roman Catholic nuns to reorganize their hospitals and their missions. And, more recently, it provides "the warm comforting presence" which Jean Waddell experienced when he strode through the door of the Evin high-security prison in Iran seven years ago, to tell her that seven months of detention could soon be at an end.

In all the now famous arm-wrestling bouts with Revolutionary Guards in Tehran or in the handshaking, back-slapping confusion of well-publicized arrivals among militia men of the Lebanon, the physical presence is inescapable but it surely accounts only partially for his prominence and his successes on the international stage. After all, there are many other men – both secular and religious – who stand six feet seven inches tall, and who so far have been denied the title of "miracle worker", ecclesiastical "trouble shooter", and "the Church of England's own Dr Kissinger". There is indeed much more to this complex man who, although he clearly enjoys the limelight, and the hyperbole of newspaper headlines, knows full well that he remains on paper, at least, nothing more dramatic than The Archbishop of Canterbury's Secretary for Anglican Communion Affairs.

A story Terry Waite tells illustrates vividly a quality which is the very reverse of that suggested by his physical stature. It tells of vulnerability, of the fragility and the value of individual life. And it is concern for them which lies at the heart of all he does.

The story dates from one of his earlier visits to Beirut when he happened to be trapped in his hotel by crossfire from opposing factions out on the streets. A rocket launcher had been set up in the front lobby, and bullets seemed to be flying everywhere. What stayed particularly in his mind was the sudden appearance of a car outside. As a man and woman drove past into view a stray bullet found its random and innocent target, and the man fell dead over the wheel. His wife rushed inside screaming, and left Terry Waite, the onlooker, wondering what, in God's name, could be done to bring about peace, understanding, and an end to the madness of warfare. It is this simple, direct feeling for the suffering of individual people which motivates Terry Waite. Simplicity of this kind, of course, rarely makes the headlines but it is precisely because it finds an expression in one so much larger than life that the phenomenon of the Church's special envoy has begun to be taken with (arguably uncharacteristic) seriousness by the world's press and television networks. Qualities which the public has only recently begun to appreciate, however, have been well-known to hundreds of men and women over the years, to people working well outside the glare of camera lights, whether in everyday parish work in Bristol in the early sixties, or in emergency relief operations in the Sudan almost a decade later.

"Obviously the successes he's had in the release of hostages have greatly depended on his ability to sit quiet and to listen. He's not one for storming in and making demands. Before Terry says anything himself he makes a point of hearing out what other people have to tell him." Rachel Moss had her first inklings of perhaps his most potent quality – that of silence – over twenty years ago, when a rather fresh-faced recruit to the Church Army (with whose misleadingly military connotations Terry Waite now feels distinctly uneasy) made his way to Bristol to help train lay people in church work. Knowing when to press forward an advantage, knowing when to hold back, and knowing, most significantly of all, when to let others take control, have been the open secrets of his success in great matters as well as small.

Rachel's husband Basil, then a priest in Bristol, explains the technique in the more down-to-earth terms Terry Waite himself used at the time. "Suppose you want the church hall redecorated. The trick is to encourage the parish to help you do it. Encourage, please note, not force! One style is for the vicar to decide what day to do it on, to decide what colour to do it out in, what volunteers will be needed, and that they will all turn up at such and such a time. No one agrees, no one disagrees – and no one turns up either, so the vicar does the decorating himself. Now the other style is to ask, 'Is it about time for a coat of paint?', 'What sort of colour scheme would suit you?', and 'How should we organize it?' That way you get your volunteers organizing themselves, and the church hall's redecorated without you really knowing how. That was Terry's style and he's carried it on ever since."

Outwardly that "style" may amount to nothing more remarkable than secular diplomacy, but inwardly it owes little to the stock-in-trade of Whitehall professionals. It springs from a deeper source. To understand Terry Waite you first have to understand that it is the Christian faith which sustains and propels him. The Book of Common Prayer, for example, has been of inestimable value to him in his self-confessed times of frustration, isolation and depression in the Middle East. It came as something of a surprise to him to discover at such times that he had unwittingly memorized whole sections of it, so that he could sit back and recite the offices of the church in circumstances far removed from the ordered calm of Lambeth Palace, where he has his base in London. Many of the Psalms, too, he knows by heart through forty-odd years of continuous use. Interviewed once in a Russian Orthodox church in London, he admitted that prayer should be "as natural an activity as breathing", something which is of another world and yet also part of this one. It is the impression he gives of someone always at ease with his faith that has earned him the distinction of being described as a "Man of God". For once it is not a journalistic excess but a simple truth, and one which has contributed to the unique credentials that have gained him access to areas of public life which would have stayed firmly closed to party politicians and career diplomats.

Terry Waite first came to general attention late in 1980 when he began the negotiations to secure the release of three British and four Iranian hostages held in Iran after the fall of the Shah and the accession to power of the Ayatollah Khomeini. Four years later Libya provided the backdrop against which he was subsequently to win the freedom of four more British hostages held in Tripoli. The next two years saw repeated journeys between Britain and the Lebanon, initially at the request of the Presbyterian Church in the United States and subsequently at that of the Roman Catholic Church. In September of 1985 the Rev. Benjamin Weir, a Presbyterian minister, was released. The following year the Roman Catholic priest, Father Lawrence Jenco, and David Jacobsen, director of the American University Hospital in Beirut, walked free, having both spent over a year in captivity at the hands of Moslem fundamentalists.

Hazardous as these missions were, they could not compare in danger and personal risk with Terry Waite's last mission to Beirut to work for the release of over a dozen western hostages held by various factions. No sooner had he arrived, against the specific advice of the Foreign Office, than the delicate procedures of discussion and negotiation appeared to go haywire. For a time it seemed that new hostages were being taken almost daily, lifted from the streets and spirited away to a variety of rooms, cellars, and secret hideaways in West Beirut. Events culminated in what many had secretly feared – the disappearance on 20th January of Terry Waite himself.

At Christmas-time, shortly before his departure, he explained something of the pain of separation and the toll his unpredictable departures had taken on his family, his wife, Frances, and his four children. Despite it all, he said, he had to continue. He saw it now as a duty. He had made a commitment to the hostages and had to see it through, although he admitted it was his most difficult trip so far and involved complexity which he had never believed would drag on so long. Once accepted, that commitment implied total involvement. It meant, he said, living with the same sorts of pressures that the families of the hostages have to live with day in, day out – the uncertainty, the vulnerability, and the frustration. After weeks of sharing the same mental anguish as the kidnappers' victims he now shared the same physical conditions – as a victim himself.

So how could it be that this dignified man of the Church, this embodiment of English courtesy and reserve, should find himself embroiled in the dirty business of hostage-taking in the chaos and anarchy of one small corner of the Middle East? To find the answer you need first to look at how the character of each mission has subtly changed.

The mission to Iran was church business. Pure and simple. Anglican missionaries were being held on implausible charges of spying. To release them was very clearly well within the brief of Mr Waite's job as the Archbishop of Canterbury's envoy. The appeal came quite specifically from members of the Anglican Communion, and as an adviser on the affairs of the Anglican Church worldwide Mr Waite was the man to go.

Success brought him celebrity. But it was not so much this which appealed to the families of the British hostages in Libya as the fact that here was a man whose simple honesty and integrity, whose independence of all political considerations, might triumph where other efforts had come to nothing. It was a direct appeal to Lambeth Palace on behalf of one British hostage, Alan Russell, a teacher and church organist, that brought Terry Waite once more into the limelight. In his dealings to date he has not been the one to make the first move. He has waited to be asked.

"The key thing is, when he starts something he has to see it through. It's a piece of advice his father gave him and Terry often repeats it." BBC journalist John Waite, his cousin and good friend over the years, knows the process well. "The problem is that he's started so many jobs it's going to be difficult for him ever to call it quits. You see, in a sense events in Iran overtook him. What people don't realize is that he gets hundreds and hundreds of requests for help, from all kinds of people. Of them only a tiny few may be held hostage, and they are the ones which hit the headlines. But every week he and his secretary go through sackfuls of letters which he answers personally. Now, in some cases just a reply will help to reassure them, in others he might telephone the person to offer help or comfort, and then again if he happens to be on a visit somewhere he will go out of his way to call on them personally to see what he can do. So, you see, events have overtaken him, and I think it's increasingly difficult for him to keep up with all the demands that are made on his time and energies. If you ever use the word 'diplomat' to him he'll laugh it away. You'll never get him to agree that this is what he is doing. I think what you would get him to agree to is that he is demonstrating Christianity in practice – concern for your fellow man, whether he happens to be an Anglican or not."

The first indication that the special envoy's role was widening was apparent in Libya. Here was a Christian representative working in a Moslem country on behalf of a mixed group of expatriates made up of a teacher, a lecturer, a telephone engineer and an oil worker, some of whom had only the loosest links with the church back home. Clearly the role of "Man of God" counted for something in paving the way to that patch of common ground on which all parties could stand, independent of national or domestic political considerations. But the cynical found it hard to swallow the package whole. After all, in the Middle East was not religion itself the cause of some of the fiercest fighting and most chilling cruelty? And could such a humble Christian man as Terry Waite ever hope to make any religious appeal which would hold water with fervent Islamic believers?

The emphasis of the appeal now shifted. It was to be described as a "humanitarian mission", a phrase and a motive acceptable to Moslem, Christian, and non-believer alike. Once he had turned this corner Terry Waite, whether he liked it or not, was clearly set on a course which would bring him into contact with scores of anxious relatives of hostages of all persuasions, seeing in him perhaps their last source of hope. As former ABC Middle East Correspondent, Charles Glass, put it, "What does the guy do? Does he turn down an appeal on behalf of Lawrence Jenco because he's not an Anglican? Or does he accept it and then turn down other appeals because the people don't happen to be Christian? I think he really has responded to humanitarian appeals and I don't doubt his sincerity at all."

All of which may explain in part why he does what he does. But HOW does he do it? In the public mind he has shot to fame as a skilled negotiator. But to think of him as such is to misunderstand the nature of the task he has set himself and which the Anglican Church endorses. He cannot negotiate; he can only mediate. Negotiators have power, mediators have none. What Terry Waite has achieved – in the Church's name – he has achieved through influence not muscle, through status not threat. True, the Iranian Mullahs, who have control over the taking and release of hostages, seem to have perfectly timed their humanitarian gesture of goodwill towards three American hostages to coincide not only with Terry Waite's mercy mission to Beirut, but also with a rather more secret deal to clinch a cargo of American armaments to Tehran. But Terry Waite, say his closest friends, could not have known of that. "He's a man totally without guile," said one, "and he's been very badly compromised by the Americans." But some of those same friends wonder how he could have been naïve enough to accept lifts between Cyprus and Lebanon on American aircraft. Whether he was unwittingly used as a convenient smokescreen to hide covert arms deals will not be known until key figures in White House circles reveal the whole truth of what negotiations took place between the United States and Iran.

In the meantime, however, what no one doubts is Terry Waite's bravery. Returning to a country where speculation and rumour about his own knowledge of events could have jeopardized not only his chances of success but his life as well, was clearly courage of a high order. Nor was that courage diminished by the fact that he himself – with his hitchhiking on US helicopters and his encounter with Colonel Oliver North – was partly responsible for that very speculation. Mediation in Beirut was, as he was reported to have said at the time, "a very dangerous business. Normally I'm taken in a car to a deserted building, usually in the night. I walk into a building alone. I'm collected by someone and blindfolded, then I'm taken to another location, and I have to conduct discussions while someone has a gun in my back."

Negotiators traditionally work in teams, have documents, and files, aides and secretaries; most of all they have something to bargain with. Terry Waite's description of his solitary, nocturnal assignations paints a somewhat different picture. Here, surely, is the classic mediator; unarmed and alone, the honest broker, there "to intervene for the purpose of reconciling" as the Oxford English Dictionary defines a role tailor-made for a man who, as one senior church diplomat put it, "Takes God seriously".

But personal danger is not the only price to pay. Another is public contempt. It may be strange, on the face of it, that the good-hearted "Christian Soldier" canonized in the popular press should incur the scorn of anyone. But it happened in 1984 during his mediation in Libya. The murder of WPC Fletcher by a gunman from the Libyan

People's Bureau in London cast a long shadow over Terry Waite's mission to Tripoli. There were many voices raised to condemn any British involvement with State-backed terrorists. There were many who claimed to be sickened by the sight of a representative of the Established Church of England sitting calmly in the Bedouin tent of a foreign leader, apparently humbling himself as he thrashed out a bargain for the release of innocent men detained unjustly by an alien regime. The incident raised many questions. Was political expediency the real reason for releasing the hostages? Could this magnanimous, "humanitarian" gesture be a suitable peace offering by the Libyan Colonel, a prelude to restoring normal relations between the two countries? And could all of it remain conveniently hidden in the background, while a harmless, neutral front man took the credit? Certainly some Middle East correspondents at the time say that Terry Waite was perfectly aware of the dangers of being used for political propaganda and successfully avoided it. Others, however, think differently.

"He's got a lot of presence," says one, "useful presence. But he's not so much a negotiator as someone who can set a scene. The Libyans watch a lot of television and they take notice when someone arrives with a bit of a flourish, so when Terry Waite flew into town – very high profile – the stage was set. Wheels began turning and an extra shove was given to the whole machinery. But he was really something of a front man. He was actually making some useful contacts there, but I know for a fact that two of the people who were absolutely key in the whole affair he never met. Ever. No, he's not so much the negotiator as . . . how would I describe him . . . the ring master in a circus. Except that he has no control over the wild animals. He arrives looking very important and the show starts. The animals start to jump through the hoops, and he doesn't realize it's got nothing to do with the whip he's cracking, nor how close the animals are to eating him." The analogy, though exaggerated, makes its point. But only partially. To pursue it: there were certainly many people in the audience at the time (and all of them safe behind the Big Top's protective bars) who would have thought at least twice before taking the place of the master of ceremonies in the arena itself and who, having paid for their ringside seats were, in the end, happy to see the animals jump at all.

Some weren't, of course; there were observers at home who thought Mr Waite should not tarnish Britain's and the Church's good name by even talking to terrorist regimes. But that is not how Terry Waite himself saw things. For him it was not Libya talking to Britain, but Colonel Gaddafi talking to Terry Waite. Man to man. In the past he had made it clear that he felt Christians should be very careful about being caught up with mass movements, about being ensnared in politics. Aware though he was that there are times when one is forced to take them into account, he went on to urge that respect for the individual be kept at the heart of our understanding. It is, he said, around the individual soul that the world turns, and where the soul brushes wings with the love of God that the meaning of life can be discovered. Small wonder, then, that he has persisted, at some cost to himself and his family, to work ceaselessly for individuals caught up in events bigger than themselves, and that he has taken his own individual and independent stand at the intersection of prayer and action to help innocent prisoners be free.

2

EARLY YEARS

When Lena Waite saw her son on television for the first time she could hardly believe it. She called in his sister Diana from the kitchen to confirm the sighting, but by the time she arrived his brief appearance was over. "But it was Terry all right," she says, "standing there at Vienna railway station checking his watch against the station clock. You couldn't miss him because he was head and shoulders above the crowd." Those who have followed his career from afar and tuned in at dramatic moments in world events to see the reassuring presence of the arch envoy, at times almost nightly, on the screen, may find Mrs Waite's surprise rather strange. Less strange perhaps when the *date* of this far from momentous broadcast is revealed. "It was on Children's Hour in about 1955. He could only have been fifteen or sixteen, no more."

What? Hostages in the Tyrol? Trouble in Central Europe? Had someone called for young Terry then? Not so, but the circumstances of the trip are revealing of the character of a solitary cyclist who was eventually to become an international globetrotter. "It was all part of a cycling holiday he'd arranged by himself", his mother recalls. "He took the train and boat to the continent and planned to cycle all round the Black Forest. All by himself. It just so happened that a new station in Vienna had opened, and they were filming it for the television. And there was Terry with his rucksack on his back standing on the platform."

The story confirms a love of travel and a restlessness that had become apparent much earlier in smaller ways. Terry Waite himself remembers the disappointment he felt when the family could not afford the fifteen pounds to send him on a school trip to France with his classmates. David, his brother, seven years Terry's junior, recalls it, too. "My dad was the village bobby and my mum didn't have a job, so with only one wage coming in they had to tell him that they just couldn't afford to send him. Terry was very, very upset about that, and felt that his big chance to travel had come and gone. It seems very ironic that now he must have gone round the world several times over, but I think that incident sort of stoked up the fires and made him determined, if this trip was going to be denied him, to make sure he went on trips later on."

Terence Hardy Waite was born on 31st May 1939 in Bollington near Macclesfield in Cheshire, the son of Lena and Thomas, a police constable. "He was quite a small baby, six pounds ten ounces, actually", says his mother. "When he was nine months old we moved to Henbury at the other side of Macclesfield, and we stayed there until he was seven, when we moved on to Styal near Wilmslow."

Although it seems likely that his formative years were spent in Styal, one key incident much earlier did determine the broad direction in which his professional life would eventually move. His mother takes up the story. "He always wanted to go to church. For as long as I can remember, even when he was a tiny boy. Our house was just five minutes away from the church just up the road, but with Diana being a baby and my husband being on duty in the Police Force I couldn't always take Terry along. But he still wanted to go, even though he wasn't quite four at the time. Well, he'd got friendly with this old man who used to go to church regularly, and who told us he would

23

call for Terry on Sunday mornings and take him along. We had a long drive and a set of double gates at the end, where Terry would wait impatiently for the man to turn up. I'd always told him to wait there and not to go through the gates until he arrived to collect him. But one Sunday he was out there waiting and waiting; the bells were ringing and there was no sign of this old man, who hadn't rung up to tell us he wasn't coming. Well, the bells rang and rang and then they stopped, so Terry thought he'd better be quick and he ran along there all by himself. And he wasn't quite four! He was the youngest child there – and all on his own. I remember, too, he was the youngest person to get a Sunday School prize. A little boy like that! I remember him walking up to the altar. He always loved the church."

By the time the family had moved to Styal Terry was already an enthusiastic member of the church choir, and was always to remember the encouragement and the advice his father gave him: "Once you start a job, stick at it until you've finished." By now Terry had a younger brother, David, who has only a dim recollection, in his early days, of being cajoled by his big brother to come and join him at the "Tin Tabernacle" where Terry was a regular worshipper. The church has since been demolished, but it exercised a powerful influence on the young Terry Waite. "I've got him to thank for my name, as a matter of fact", says David. "I was born on a Sunday, when Terry was a youngster trotting off to church. He came back this particular Sunday to find he had a brother. I was premature, as it turned out, and my parents thought I was going to die that day, so they felt they had to get me christened as soon as possible. They brought the vicar in but they hadn't any names planned. So then Terry barges in straight back from Sunday School where he'd been learning the story of David and Jonathan. So he very kindly comes up with this suggestion and my parents agreed. So here I am. David John Waite. But I must say I'm ever so grateful he hadn't been listening to the story of David and Goliath!"

The family was not a particularly religious one according to David, and it was something of a mystery where Terry got his yearning from. "I don't think for one minute my father would have said he was a Christian in the sense I understand the term now. My mother had a strong faith, but I think it tends to be the case sometimes that when one partner in a marriage doesn't appear to have that faith, the other partner sort of drops away in order to keep the peace maybe or just because it isn't possible to worship together. I think that's what happened in our family. I can't, as a child, remember Mum actually attending church very often. Maybe the odd time, but not regularly."

Being brought up in a settled community played an important part in the lives of both David and Terry, who has since looked back on it as a profound and valuable experience. It was perhaps the stable base – like his own family today – to which he unerringly returned after his day-long expeditions by bike around Cheshire and Staffordshire. The bike he managed to buy from the proceeds of a newspaper round, and he used it to travel as far and as widely as he could. One of the many paradoxes which make up Terry Waite was apparent even then. Day after day he would take himself off into the solitude of, say, the Peak District, clocking up hundreds of miles on his bicycle, and yet his capacity for enjoying the company of others seemed a perfect match for this solitary nature.

He made friends wherever he went. One day, for instance, he came home to surprise his mother with the disclosure that he had flown over the house that day. When Lena Waite had adjusted to the shock she had no difficulty extracting the story from him. "He'd got on his bike and decided to cycle off to Manchester Airport, and he'd happened to get friendly with a man who had a little plane. He offered to take Terry up in it and sure enough he agreed, and that was how he came to be flying over the police house in Styal that day. He used to take him up quite a lot until one Saturday – when fortunately Terry hadn't gone along – he crashed and was killed. But that was typical of Terry. Always making friends wherever he went. And yet in many ways he was a very shy boy. He spent a lot of his time reading and listening to the radio. Not that he was a recluse or anything like that. He could be quite boisterous – climbing trees and all that sort of thing." A curious hobby at the time, she recalls, was stiltwalking. "He made these stilts and, as if he wasn't tall enough already, used to enjoy teetering around on them making himself even bigger!"

To David he was always an excellent and exciting companion. "You've got to remember he's seven years older than me, and so he was at an age when he could do things which were well beyond my scope. But sometimes he would take me on a trip to Manchester by train. He'd be telling stories of bike rides he'd been on or adventures he'd got involved in, he'd be pointing things out along the way, and making up a plan of action for when we got into Manchester. So even the most basic railway journey would be a terrific excitement with him. He just had a way of making life stimulating and full of incident, so that when you were with him you sort of got this charge from him."

Despite his capacity for seriousness and solitude, the young Terry Waite was not exactly averse to the odd childish prank – a hazardous tendency and one which was not always wise for the eldest son of the village policeman. "I remember on one occasion in winter," his brother recalls, "it had been alleged (that's the term, isn't it?) that a snowball had been posted through someone's letterbox, and I don't think it was ever actually proved that Terry did it but he was certainly with the group that did. When I say he used to go about in a 'gang' today's connotations throw up the wrong image, but there were a few of them who used to go about together, and being high-spirited lads they could occasionally get up to a bit of mischief. The thing was that they'd all scuttle away to hide, but when somebody looked out of the window they'd inevitably see this one boy standing shoulder high above the rest. And so they'd immediately come rushing round to our house, complaining to my parents that they'd seen such and such a thing happening, and although they couldn't be sure who all the culprits were, 'One of them', they would say to my father, 'is your son'. And it was most embarrassing for my dad, being the upholder of law and order!"

Thomas Waite himself was, according to David, a great disciplinarian. "He had very definite rules for us, and I think we were all a bit scared of him really. His attitude was that as a police family there were always standards we had to uphold. I think Terry was always aware of having a father who represented law and order. But I think also that came partly from living in a police house. You see, it wasn't separate; it was actually attached to the police station, so very often 'criminals', or what have you, who had been taken into custody, would wander into our house for one reason or another. I can remember one occasion when we were all supposed to be going out for the day and – this often happened – we were all sitting there ready for the off when the phone rang and my dad took it. The next minute he was back in the room and said, 'Sorry, kids, it's off'. And the sheer disappointment of it I can still remember to this day. There was the time, for instance, when we were all set for a day's outing when my dad had to go out. The trip was cancelled and he actually brought a man back to the house. He took him out into the garden, sat him in one of our deckchairs, and gave him a drink. It turned out that he had tried to commit suicide in Styal woods but somebody had reported the incident and my dad took charge. So those were the kinds of situations Terry and I were brought up with. And we were always taught, or rather we somehow knew by instinct, that what you heard in the home was never to be repeated. And I'm sure that stood Terry in good stead, because I'm absolutely positive that any confidence given to him will not be broken. It was instilled in us from a very, very early age. Terry would never break that."

The picture of the stern and disapproving father, however, is so far one-sided, and David concedes that other qualities were of equal influence on both him and Terry – qualities of fair-mindedness and of paternal concern which flowed from a warm and tender heart. His father remained a constable all his life, establishing himself as a reliable, well-liked, and well-respected member of a stable community which Terry Waite himself so values today. As an indication of how the father's reputation has lived on, David remembers a recent visit to Styal with his mother. It was forty years ago, aged seven, that he left the house to up-sticks again for another police house in Thelwall, outside Lymm in Cheshire. Although he had not been back to Styal for over a decade, when he did return, he discovered the old house empty but still referred to by those old enough to remember as "the Waite House".

"My father's attitude was not always to be getting more and more convictions. In his day, the more convictions you got the quicker you progressed up the ladder but he wasn't like that. He took the view that if you could warn people or caution them you could stop them doing something, without having to go through the courts. And he felt it was far better for them – of course it didn't earn him any stars but it did win him a lot of respect.

"So the warm-hearted man and the disciplinarian went hand in hand, and both Terry and I appreciated that, I think. It's certainly influenced the way I treat my children, for example. Nobody is more secure than when they have boundaries in which they know they can work. Terry and I knew that we were safe within a certain boundary, but that if we went beyond it then we were liable to come under the wrath of our father."

Throughout these early years twin qualities seemed to be developing in Terry Waite, which developed side by side and seemed to complement each other. On the one hand he had the great capacity for reflection while still, on the other, retaining a sense of fun and sense of action. He was popular among his school contemporaries, and made an excellent head boy at Stockton Heath Secondary Modern School where, as he confessed later, he grew rather impatient with his studies. He longed to be out and about, and already had half an eye on a career in the Forces being, even in those early days, he says, strongly patriotic. It seems to have been a fairly uneventful school career, with the young Terry involving himself in all the usual pursuits a schoolboy would – cricket, tennis, swimming, and of course the bike. The headmaster told Mrs Waite that here was a child who, with his exam results, really should have gone to the Grammar School but, she recalls, "it was a good school, he liked it there and so he just stayed on."

All the while, though, another far from ordinary quality in one so young was making itself more apparent. His already strong Christian faith was maturing to a degree which was later to make a profound impression on older and more experienced clergy and lay people all over the world. Christianity was beginning to be something which he took with the utmost seriousness, and yet which he carried with him in the most natural of ways. He was at home with his faith, and the faith had found a strong and ready servant. An incident related by his younger brother illustrates some of this maturity and seriousness, coupled with a complete lack of self-consciousness.

"We shared a room at home, and one night I remember him coming in to tell me he had been to a meeting somewhere, and he'd experienced something which had touched him deeply. Now whether this was the point at which he was, for want of a better word, converted, I don't know. But I recall him telling me – a young lad of seven or eight or so – that God had touched his life in some way, and that if I ever wanted to make that kind of step he would be there to help me. And he would be able to tell me what I should do. He used to pray silently by the side of the bed in the evening, and I know he was very fond of the Prayer Book. I, of course, was a typical, horrible younger brother, and many a time I would ask him why he was bothering to pray because there was no one there."

Should anyone suspect that the ease with which Terry Waite habitually discusses his faith in front of the microphones and the television cameras of the world's media is part of a carefully honed public relations strategy there, surely, is proof to the contrary: in the picture of the young adolescent kneeling in silent devotion, patiently resistant to the childish taunts of his young brother, mature beyond his years and basing all he did (and does) on the bedrock of the Gospel message.

But a footnote to those who fear for David's salvation! Some of the influence of the older brother certainly rubbed off onto the younger but led them both along quite separate avenues of formal worship. Where David tends to the "low" church, Pentecostal form, Terry is more at home in "high", Anglo-Catholic traditions. The formal structures of the Orthodox Church he finds particularly appealing. The traditions that stretch back over the centuries, with the icons representing the great figures in the life of the Church, the candles representing the ever-present light of God, even in what seem the most hopeless times, exert a strong and enduring attraction. Indeed he has often lamented the disappearance of much of the tradition in Anglican worship, regretting that to enter some Anglican churches nowadays is not really to know where you are any more, because of the changes and variations in the liturgy. The Orthodox liturgy, on the other hand, gives him a known fixed point, a link with generations of believers and a discipline within which he can be free. It echoes David's earlier observation that security could be found within distinct boundaries – the lesson that their father taught them both.

"Another thing our father taught us," says David, "was never to look down on anyone and never to be over-awed by anyone either. We were taught to respect everybody whatever their station in life – whether the grandest man in the village or a tramp in the street." Recent events have proved that he has retained the advice. No one who has seen Terry Waite with world figures one moment and with down-and-outs at the Crisis at Christmas charity appeals the next, can doubt that. "Our dad was a man of great wisdom really. And Terry picked up a lot from him. Honesty, dependability, trustworthiness, discretion. Dad never talked about his work to us much, just as Terry doesn't reveal much of what goes on in all his missions."

Two of the faults which David, Terry himself, and those close to him do admit to, however, are impatience and a temper. "He's tolerant up to a point," says David, "and then the fuse goes. He'll go red in the face and stalk off somewhere, waving his arms about. It will be a big explosion while it lasts but all over fairly quickly. But over the years he's learnt to keep his emotions in check which, I suppose, is part of his professionalism. If you are going to do that sort of job you have to do that really, don't you?"

Indeed, I and other journalists – gathered at Lambeth Palace some months ago for what was to be a routine press conference – had the opportunity to witness something of that side of his nature at first hand. The waiting reporters had expected him to announce his departure for South Africa in the next few days to monitor, as an independent church observer, the deteriorating conditions in the townships as the rioting grew heavier. We sat back, only half attentively waiting for the predictable itinerary, until without warning the mood of the moment changed. Terry Waite had been effectively denied a visa for the period of time he needed it and was, he announced, "very angry". Little of it showed on his face, but one sensed great currents of it below the surface. It is an observation corroborated by his former mentor in his early days as a Bristol lay worker, Laurence Reading. "His anger is deep down. He finds it hard to get angry, but it's there all right."

But there is, of course, a lightness of touch to Terry Waite's approach to people and to his work. And that, too, goes side by side with his serious nature. An illustration from his brother, David: "The circumstances of his confirmation were, to say the least, rather unusual, and I think they're quite indicative of the things that have made him what he is. Styal church was a kind of outpost from the main church in Wilmslow, and so it didn't have a hall to go with it. They had to rent out rooms for various activities, and the room they hired for the confirmation classes was above a pub, "The Ship Inn". Terry always used to say that he was glad this had been the arrangement. Too often, he felt, religion could be divorced from the normal cut and thrust of everyday life, and the fact that they were studying over a public bar brought into focus the nearness of spiritual life with the everyday. The men downstairs were laughing and joking and drinking, while quite different celebrations were going on above them. It was a good balance to have the jollity filtering through to the confirmation class and anchoring it to the day-to-day world. I was listening to 'Songs of Praise' the other day on BBC television, and they were singing the hymn, 'All Creatures that on Earth do Dwell', and it struck me that the idea of 'singing to the Lord with cheerful voice' and 'serving Him with mirth' are very much part of Terry's make-up. He has a very rich sense of humour which is not always apparent when he's being circumspect about his missions. But it's there all right, that jovial side to him."

I wondered if as a boy David had had any intimation of greatness in Terry, any inkling that great things lay in store. "I've always looked up to him, and he's always seemed to me rather unreachable and out of the ordinary, but I'd really no idea he'd be doing the sort of work he is doing, but it was clear from early on that he was going to travel."

His first attempt at that, however, got him no further than the railway station. Growing impatience with academic studies (which he was later to resume, and somewhat regret having prematurely abandoned) led him to consider a career where travel and adventure would be the keynotes. He thought about the navy but his parents were set against it. This, as David recalls, led to a "great debate" in the household and a degree of tension in the air. But Terry was determined to go and, armed with his railway ticket, made his way to Styal station accompanied by a disapproving but tolerant mother. "The train pulled in. He put his hand on the carriage door and I said to him, 'Well, are you going or not?' and he paused a moment, looked at me and said, 'No, I'm not'. And he came back with me." Lena Waite laughs now at the story, but there was clearly much relief that her sixteen-year-old son had resisted the call of the sea. "He said how glad he was that he hadn't gone after all, but he was still very unsettled, and at seventeen he decided to join up with the Grenadier Guards." His parents agreed to his wishes and there was no turning back from the Caterham-bound train this time.

But things did not turn out smoothly and the longed-for career got off to a false start. His mother continues the story. "He hadn't had his uniform on for long when he started to come out in this rash all over his body, and he was put in the military hospital for a long, long period until they finally sent him home. Then after he'd been up here for a while in civvies the rash started to disappear. So the doctor thought everything was fine and sent Terry back. No sooner had he had his uniform on for a couple of days than he started to come down with the complaint yet again. Eventually they tumbled to it, and realized it was the dye in the khaki which was causing the problem. Terry was allergic to it, and because of a small thing like that he had to come out. As a matter of fact he got a tiny pension because he'd been in. for a few weeks before being 'invalided out'."

The five-month period spent in the military hospital was a formative one for Terry Waite. It was an opportunity for quiet and for reflection. For many young men of his age it could have been an opportunity missed, but it found a welcome echo in his own serious personality. He seriously considered the Church as an option and considered (but eventually rejected) the possibility of the ordained ministry. The allergy had not diminished his urge for variety and adventure which he thought a settled parish life would prevent. His next career move, though once again it took the family by surprise, eventually won their full approval. Terry decided to join up with and train for the Church Army – the social and evangelistic arm of the Church of England. The uniform did not have khaki dye in it, which may have been one advantage, but there was far more to his decision than that, and it was one which was to set the seal on his professional life ahead.

Before leaving this transitional stage, though, to move on to Terry Waite's middle years, allow David to make an observation which perhaps only a brother can, and to see in that lengthy period of recuperation and reflection in a military hospital a poignant counterpart to Terry's latest period of immobility and detention. When I spoke to David Terry had been missing, presumed kidnapped, for over a month. The concern told in his voice and yet he was still hopeful – certain that God was in full control, that God would remain faithful to him in the time of trial, and that Terry himself would be drawing strength from that presence. "We pray with the children at night for Terry's safe return, we pray he will come out of it all unscathed. But if we go back to that time in the hospital I think we can see some parallels with the current situation. I honestly believe that what he's going through now will be a similar period of reflection for him. I think he will come out of it a different man than when he went in. I think some of the rough corners will have rubbed off him a bit and some of that restless energy may be tamed. Maybe he'll calm down a bit more. That energy's been put to good use but maybe he just needs to slow it down a bit and take life a little more gently. I don't think either of us is particularly emotional. We both have deep feelings but tend not to show them.

And I suppose in general we're not a very demonstrative family. But there is a bond between us. In the recent past when we've been through difficult times I've dropped a line to Terry and he's been straight back with a word of support and encouragement. I suppose it's the typical stiff-upper-lip British thing not to say what you feel about someone until he's in a tight situation, but I'm very fond of him and I think he is of me. And I do feel that this period will be crucial in his life. Whatever happens will affect him deeply, as it will us all."

3

CHRISTIAN SOLDIER

"Terry Waite is the world's best-known Church Army Officer." The opening words of his outline biography from the Church Army's archives are true enough. But there are many who would find it hard to resist adding an ironic (but equally true) footnote along the lines of: "But very few people realize it!"

Captain Gordon Kitney, CA, his friend and fellow recruit of almost thirty years ago, puts it differently, "We've all said on occasions, 'Why the heck doesn't he SAY he's a member of the Church Army!' But then when we came to understand that in some Arabic dialects this could be translated as 'Church Militia' we started to see that in the present circumstances it's quite reasonable for him not to use it for fear of creating entirely the wrong impression." Terry Waite does not use the title "Captain" and rarely wears Church Army uniform these days, having come to question the appropriateness of military-sounding titles in the contemporary work of the Church.

But styles have changed. In the late 1950s while he was recuperating in an army hospital in the Home Counties, wondering where his future lay, the Society's military ring, with the promise of the adventure prematurely denied him in the Guards by his allergy, had a distinct appeal. He first came into contact with the Church Army at the Caterham depot, where for many years it had run a canteen, and where generations of young men would have doubtless been attracted as much by the billiard table and the free and easy atmosphere as by the discreet and enduring Christian witness it represented in the camp. Church Army men would help out in chaplain's duties, say matins and evensong, visit families in time of need, and do the hospital rounds, during which, though he had never heard of the organization before, Terry Waite became attracted to the variety and seriousness of purpose of this branch of the Church of England's work. It was the practical side of it, he was later to say, which appealed to him, the strong and visible pastoral concern for people, whether in residential homes for the sick and elderly, or emergency hostels for down-and-outs, or, then again, in itinerant mission work throughout villages, towns and cities the length and breadth of the land. Earlier, while still a serviceman, he had, as the Church Army archive reports, "felt the first stirrings of vocation". These would certainly take him into the Church in one way or another but by themselves would not necessarily point the way at what was decidedly a crossroads in his adult life. Earlier he had considered the monastic life, visiting the Community of the Resurrection at Mirfield, in Yorkshire, but had come to the conclusion that the celibate life and the ordained ministry were not for him. The Church Army was.

In 1958 he made the first formal move, taking himself off to the Selection Conference where potential recruits would be chosen for training. Individual interviews with the college principal, discussion groups among other hopeful contemporaries, visits to hostels, invitations to speak in public and talk in private to the residents one met, and, most of all, a thorough search of a person's Christian faith and motives, formed the core of the rigorous procedure for selecting the new intake. Once he had satisfied the selectors of his willingness and his aptitude Terry Waite, along with twenty-three other young men of the class of '58, made his way to 1–5 Cosway Street, W1 – the Church Army Training College off the Marylebone Road in central London, where two years of study and training were about to begin.

Gordon Kitney, who had joined the year before, remembers rumours circulating at the time of this impressive man from the Guards about to join them. "A recruit from the services was always a pleasure and something to look forward to. In a way they counteracted the large number of Billy Graham converts who'd come to Christ in the early sixties as a result of the evangelistic rallies and crusades organized in Britain at the time. Not that we minded the Billy Graham people one bit – the Church Army tries to steer a middle course and appeal to all – but many of them had not had church associations before, and I suppose it was nice to be welcoming someone who had some familiarity with the traditions of the Church already. And someone with a degree of maturity who'd already been about a bit."

Although Terry Waite had turned his back on the ascetic, religious life his conditions of Christian service were far from luxurious. Compared to today, at least, this was an age of austerity – and even more so in the Church's training colleges, which frequently modelled themselves on the religious communities and their monastic traditions. He was assigned to the typical, spartan study/bedroom with nothing more than its gas fire, bookcase, chest of drawers, table, chair, wardrobe and bed. Lighting the fire in the mornings to dress or pray by was frowned on, considered, as Gordon Kitney says, "unholy", and accordingly training officers would do their morning rounds to ensure that sensual excess of this kind was discouraged. The early morning bell would ring at 6.30, summoning all the students to a day of order and routine.

After washing each would be responsible for stripping his bed and preparing the room to conform to strict standards of spotless propriety. Morning prayer was at 7.30 after which, at 8 o'clock, was breakfast. These twenty minutes were spent in silence by way of training all the young men (and women, who ate separately) to communicate without speaking. Gordon Kitney remembers how brown and white bread were deliberately set out on separate plates at either end of the table, thus encouraging them all to hone down their own particular brand of mimetic communication to a spare degree of refinement. "It was hard luck, though," he says, "if you were in the middle of the table and the bread you were after was half a mile away. Then you'd have to dig somebody in the ribs. If it was Terry you'd have to be very careful where you elbowed him or you might find yourself ending up with the marmalade instead." After breakfast it was back to the rooms for half an hour of meditation and Bible reading before the day began.

The evening routine was just as sparse. There was silence from ten in the evening until nine in the morning. True, some of the students had found it possible to communicate by notes, and to circumvent the lights-out rule with torches, a margin of flexibility to the otherwise inflexible rules. But rules they were and rules they stayed – though queried at times by Terry and his contemporaries. An added inconvenience for him, though, was the size of the bed. His friends at the time remember him sending a verse from Isaiah to the college matrons, "the bed is too short for him which sleepeth upon it", a typically endearing way of ensuring that the college invested in a bed large enough to accommodate all of his body and not just part of it.

The day's study threw up its further share of Church Army idiosyncrasies. This was at a time, according to

Captain Kitney, when Church Army men, if travelling, say, on a bus, were expected to get off if a Church Army sister happened to board. The sexes, though trained together, rarely mixed. In class the men were arranged at the front, the women at the back to avoid distractions. Gordon and Terry found the only safe way of communicating with the opposite sex was to leave notes discreetly between the pages of a borrowed library book. Study quarters were firmly divided off, the men separated from the women by the so-called "Iron Curtain" hanging from a rail in the middle of the corridors on every floor. Needless to say, entrance to the college was through separate doors.

All the while the studies continued. Essays on the New and Old Testaments, Church history, textual criticism, and study of the pastoral needs of the time, all formed part of the two theological courses the Church Army in those days ran. Terry studied the more intellectually demanding of the two courses on offer, and is remembered by the then College Principal, Prebendary Donald Lynch, as "a good solid student, not especially outstanding, but a person who gave attention and enthusiasm to all he did and who brought flair to the practical pastoral work of the time."

Every minute of the college day was accounted for. Lectures in the morning, study periods in the evening, and parish work two days a week, meant that only on Monday afternoons was there any scheduled time for recreation – football or cricket in Regent's Park. There was occasionally the opportunity to go out on the town, but with only twelve shillings (sixty pence) a week from the College to get by on, such opportunities were severely restricted. David Beardshaw, a contemporary of Terry's, has vivid memories of his marvellous sense of economy: "He became supremely adept at nosing out free entertainment." The two of them made an unlikely couple

41

walking down the Edgware Road with a few pence in their pockets, ready to make an impact on the London scene. At five foot three inches tall, David Beardshaw (now a vicar in Coventry) provided a stark contrast with his twenty-year-old companion. The difference in height was exaggerated by their habit of walking together, with Terry on the pavement and David in the road. Add to that their occasional eccentricity of wearing bowler hats and carrying rolled up umbrellas, and the effect was one of a couple of escapees from the freaks' tent at P. T. Barnum's. Terry's sense of fun again!

Taking off to one's relatives for a short break was a tried and tested way of eking out the twelve shilling allowance, and Terry was often a guest at David's family home in the village of Oughtibridge outside Sheffield. While David's mother would talk about (and fondly remember) the night she went up into Terry's room to drape an eiderdown over the two bare feet which were protruding as usual from their standard-sized bed, David calls to mind an equally vivid moment. "He had this habit of just darting off at a moment's notice, on a whim. Once while he was at our home he said to me, 'Oh, I'll just nip off home to see if there's any post'. 'Home' at this time was thirty-odd miles away in Lymm in Cheshire, but up he got to hitchhike to his mother's and be back at our house for tea-time. Rather strange that, isn't it?"

Terry mixed well with his fellow students and was always good company in team games or social evenings, but even then Gordon Kitney noticed the solitary, more reflective side to his nature. "He made friends very easily but there were always moments when he seemed to want to go off on his own and think things through. He's always been involved with missions here and there and got on fine with other people, but he would frequently take himself off

on long walks across London – into churches, into the
British Museum studying biblical archaeology or what
have you. He took a great interest in what was happening
in the world at large, particularly in Africa, and was
always, in his discussions with us, homing in on places
where there was suffering and unrest in the world. He
would go off and read a lot, not because he was unsociable,
far from it, but because, as we all recognized then, he
simply needed quiet times to reflect on things." It was a
quality which Bishop Oliver Tomkins, who gave Terry
Waite his first job in Bristol in 1964, was later to recognize
and to value. "The quality", as he put it, "of being able to
look inward in order to look outward."

But life off the Marylebone Road in those days had its
lighter moments, and many of these were at Terry's own
lodgings in the Church Army's annexe away from the main
college. His room was above a pub, "The Walworth
Arms", behind the Moorfields Eye Hospital, but in contrast to "The Ship Inn" where his confirmation classes had
been held in Styal much earlier, there was no jollity
filtering up from the public bar. During his time there the
pub remained firmly shut, and the reason behind this
strange phenomenon paints an interesting picture of the
religious climate and public attitude of the time. The area
was at the centre of considerable church activity. Mission
work on the streets, loyal "high church" attendance in the
neighbourhood, and the strong presence of both the
Salvation Army and the Church Army (each with a staunch
tradition of temperance) brought pressure to bear on the
landlord of "The Yorkshire Stingo", a well-known pub
nearby. In anticipation of the imminent closure of the
"Stingo" – a much loved watering hole – it was decided to
open another, "The Walworth Arms", not a million miles
away. It was to be of no avail. The pub was destined never

to pull a single pint. The religious societies had their way and the drinkers had to go elsewhere. So the jollity that could be heard on occasions from above "The Walworth Arms" came not from bar room revellers but from the friends of Terry Waite enjoying sing-songs round the pianola and that other speciality of the house – baked beans, toast and fry-ups provided by a jovial mine host who had discovered that by turning the electric fire on its side you could rig up a rudimentary (if hazardous) form of camp cuisine to feed the troops and prolong the entertainment.

The fun is corroborated by his younger brother David, who more than once came down to London to stay with Terry in his student days. "It was a strange flat he had, now I come to think of it. To get from one part to the next the quick way was to go out onto the skylight. Quite often someone would report having seen the outline of a large man prowling across the roof! We ate very simple student-type food but he always served it up with such relish and style that you felt it was a real occasion. It may only have been cheese on toast – I know it sounds silly to say it – but I would think of it as a really tremendous banquet. He always made an effort to do things in the grand way."

By this time Terry Waite was beginning to establish himself as someone who could communicate directly and effectively the truths of the Christian faith. Part of the Church Army training, for example, involved a compulsory session at Speakers' Corner in Hyde Park, where students were expected to get across the Christian message to a largely disinterested or positively antagonistic audience. They would go in a group of a dozen or so and attempt to attract themselves a crowd. Their own group had a particularly effective though unintentional method of achieving this. One of their number was so paralysed by nerves and fear of speaking in public that he habitually fainted before mounting the soap-box, and so succeeded in generating, at a stroke, a collection of idle rubber-necks and a few genuinely concerned to help. Another student would then mount the platform, now assured of a ready-made audience, and begin. When Terry took to the soap-box looking, according to the diminutive Gordon Kitney, "like the statue of Lord Nelson", he would be quick to refer to the everyday expressions of a secular culture to make his religious point. Across the way from Speakers' Corner was the Odeon, Marble Arch, and often he would use the current film, whose title stood out in huge red letters, to make an observation. "Cat on a Hot Tin Roof", for example, might be used as an illustration of the discomfort of sin in God's good kingdom. Occasionally a tomato or an egg would hit its target, but history does not record whether Terry Waite was on the receiving end. Certainly he did come in for his fair share of heckling but friends of the time say he coped with those more than adequately.

All this was part of the daily training of the students. The forays into public speaking would be followed by forays into public houses, distributing the *Church Army Gazette* and collecting for charity. The young Terry Waite, according to reports, managed to fill his tin quickly as a result of his ready banter and genuine rapport with the people he met. There were "fishing trips" along the Edgware Road, that is to say, evangelizing in groups of two and inviting people along to Sunday worship at the headquarters church in Brunswick Street, followed, perhaps, by a slide show or a talk. Occasionally there might be hymn-singing in a pub with a friendly and receptive landlord, and Gordon Kitney has fond memories of one such place at the Angel, Islington, where a resident skiffle group provided the accompaniment.

It was typical of Terry to carry his faith and his concern with him wherever he went, and these he wore so lightly that they have become today a natural part of his personality. They were part of it even then, as Gordon Kitney can testify. "Take the time when we were having a game of cricket in the park. Now he'd be as good humoured as the rest of us – telling the batsman to expect a slow ball, then racing to the wicket and letting fly with his windmill arms. We didn't have cricket helmets then – just the odd tin helmet from our National Service days! Or perhaps, as he bowled, he'd make a comment to distract the batsman's attention – 'Mind that pigeon', he'd say just before successfully clean-bowling the man who for a moment had taken his eye off the ball. But then again there was always the serious side to him. I remember once that he was fielding on the boundary and a tramp was sitting on a bench behind him. He just forgot the game, sat next to him and started talking to the man, completely oblivious to the possibility of the opposition scoring fours. He always had this concern for people."

Concern for people. It is a quality which time and again friends and colleagues, lay and clergy from every part of the world, have noticed immediately about Terry Waite. It is a quality hard to define but, once experienced, never forgotten. I myself have had a vague intimation of it on the occasions I have met and interviewed the man. Whether in the quiet of Lambeth Palace or in the chaos of a hurried Heathrow press conference, he radiates a concern for the person he is currently talking to. "Getting on" with people, liking them for who they are, is a much understated quality, a translucent quality which adds an extra lustre to all the other more demonstrative traits a person possesses. It is, moreover, that simple, hugely impressive quality which the Archbishop's envoy has in plenty. "He would never think ill of anyone. Never do anything to hurt someone", says Gordon Kitney. "At College there'd be the usual sorts of mischief and so on. You'd go back and find your room stripped of furniture, or someone would put a cake of black face soap in your toilet bag. But Terry didn't approve of that, he wasn't at all easy with practical jokes, and found himself impatient or annoyed with the kind of humour which was hurtful or degrading to others. He's always honest and open with people." It was from this time on that people of all ages, backgrounds, abilities and persuasions became the focal point of everything he did.

Outsiders may be forgiven for looking at the Church of England today and thinking they see in it a full spectrum of separate Christian denominations rather than any one unified body of believers. But things were not so different thirty years ago. The great strength of the Church Army was that it managed to appeal to everybody – "high" or "low", "Anglo-Catholic" or "Evangelical". In practical terms, for students like Gordon Kitney, it meant initially some degree of tension. "Some of the new intake had come over from the Church of Ireland and they couldn't understand people like Terry and me who tended towards 'high church' worship. They used to push all sorts of tracts through our door, thinking somehow we were Roman Catholic. There'd be others from the Evangelical end who couldn't believe we were truly Christian if we couldn't stand up and declare that on such and such a day we were converted. So in the early days there was bound to be a shade of unease. I remember, for instance, when we went into the chapel for the first time we thought the furniture removers had been in. We'd never seen a church so bare. There was an altar, a Cross, two candlesticks, and rows and rows of wooden chairs, and that was it. But as time went on we began to accept each other's differences and see the strengths that were in each other's experience of the Christian faith."

One has only to look at Terry Waite's career to see that tolerant philosophy borne out. He has worked for the whole Church not parts of it. And his experience has given him a particular view of true Ecumenism. For him church unity does not mean sinking one's differences overnight into some common pool from which no one can draw benefit; it does not mean abandoning one's traditions in order to merge in a way which is recognizable to no one. What it does mean is understanding and openness, co-operation between traditions, good will among denominations which may still retain their individual characteristics in ways which can enrich us all. He has often spoken of his love of travel. For him not only is it a way of experiencing different cultures at close quarters, it is also a means of understanding the richness of God's creation in all its variety. Over the years, he has said, as he grows gently and confidently into his own faith, he has learnt to feel at ease with others who may express their faith in different ways. Not only that, having a faith oneself gives one no cause at all to be afraid of other different faiths that people hold. In this way travel can truly broaden the mind and deepen one's understanding of God's purpose in the world.

So let us resume at the point where the real travelling began for Terry Waite. To do this we need to pause for a moment to picture a bygone era. It is just over a quarter of a century ago, and yet it seems to belong more to the lost but half-familiar world of Thomas Hardy than to the second half of the twentieth century. Imagine if you will a two-wheeled cart boarded at the side and piled high with camping gear for a month-long expedition. At the front a long pole extends a few feet forwards, and a crossbar provides an anchor point for two young men to push. Straps are fixed to the crossbar and pulled by two more men further ahead, to give added traction uphill, and these are trailed behind the cart during descents to provide the braking power. This is the Church Army trek-cart, pushed, pulled, man-handled in all weathers by a team of eight during the month-long summer missions around the country. Gordon Kitney explains.

"Once a year the students would do what was called their 'summer work'. They would set off from a cathedral town and walk from village to village, the cart stuffed full of their belongings. At each stopping point they would knock on doors, distribute leaflets, organize events and help as much as they could in the local parish. In the evening there would be mission services open to all, with singing and prayer and then, in the morning, there would be a final service before setting off for the next spot. Once Terry himself had been commissioned, completed his training and qualified as a Church Army officer, he himself would train people to organize the treks. Conditions were pretty basic, mind you. More often than not you'd sleep in church halls, you'd find your bedding had been gnawed by the mice when you got back, and you'd frequently stay overnight in villages where there was no proper plumbing – just water from the well. Bathing would involve several trips to the pump and a delicate operation of shoe-horning yourself into the church hall sink. It was all part of the discipline. Terry enjoyed it all immensely – as we all did – and, it goes without saying, of course, he got on well with everybody he met."

The summer treks culminated in beach missions at such seaside towns as Margate, Shanklin or Cleethorpes, which would mark the end of the two-hundred-mile trail. It all seems an age away. But compare relative dates and you will discover it is not. While Terry Waite was working for the Church Army, for example, John Lennon was training at Liverpool College of Art, both of them poised to witness the dawning of an age less innocent than the last. The *Robin* comic, sister paper of the *Eagle*, organized its entertainments on the beach while Church Army officers unloaded their cart and set up shop, in friendly rivalry, along the sands dispensing puppet theatre, organizing games and plays, and discreetly, responsibly promoting the Christian faith. Times have changed.

In retrospect (though some, like Prebendary Donald Lynch, the College's principal, could see it coming already) there was an elegaic feel to those days. Society was changing fast, and mission work had to adapt to the transformation or fail. "The York Van", Terry's first posting after being commissioned, embodied perhaps the last expression of the old approach. A new era was beginning.

The van was a caravan moored semi-permanently in a parish, to which a couple of Church Army officers were attached. Here was a base for the men who lived and slept in the caravan but who, with the aid of a compliant farmer's tractor, could be towed around the area and deposited in another parish until it was time to move on again somewhere else in the York diocese. The work was much the same as that on the treks, but done with perhaps a shade more seriousness than on the one-night stop-overs. It involved Church Army people being in the mainstream of everyday life — visiting houses and hospitals, going into schools, helping the local vicar with his pastoral work in all sorts of ways. In Terry's case it meant on one occasion, so the story goes, lending a helping hand as a human tape measure. There happened to be no one around to dig the grave for a forthcoming burial, so the team volunteered, and as they had no measure asked Terry to leap down to give them an idea of when they had dug six feet. Normally, though, the duties they were assigned were more serious, involving, to a large extent, work as formal evangelists to a parish. Their varied training had given them an idea of where best their aptitudes might lie and now, for a short time while he was attached to the York van, it was clear to Terry where his future ministry lay.

"A lot of people think Terry's ordained," says Gordon Kitney, "but he had, even at the time I was training with him, made the conscious decision to work as a layman. I think he felt that all too often people assume that ministry equals clergy, and overlook the vital role non-ordained, ordinary members of a parish can have. The sole ministry of the Church isn't just up front in the sanctuary, there's as important a ministry in the world outside. I think both of us wanted to work with people in such a way that we didn't stand out. The danger, if you wear a dog-collar, is that you're immediately put on some sort of pedestal — whereas when either of us knocked on a door in those days we were just as likely to have been mistaken for the gasman. Many's the time we've been doing our rounds when the lady of the house would open the door to us and show us the gas meter!

"I would never describe Terry as an ambitious man as such. What he has done has always been for other people. But I think he is ambitious in the sense of wanting lay people to express and to be able to communicate their faith. He's anxious to enable people to reach out a hand to those who are OUTSIDE the Church, to bring people into what he's called 'a living fellowship'. He has a vision of the Church as the fellowship of ALL believers. There's nothing particularly new in that as it stands, it's as old as the

gospels themselves, but he put so much effort and enthusiasm into making the vision a reality. He was, in-
cidentally, always very aware that a lot of the work done
with lay people in a parish involved youngish or middle-
aged people, and that the elderly somehow got overlooked.
And in just the same way that he could appeal to the very
young he could also appeal to the very old. He had a great
understanding of the quality of prayer that the elderly
could offer. So he would spend a great deal of time talking
to them, making them feel an integral part of the parish
system. He appreciated the fact that, although they
couldn't take part in visiting the sick or in all the other
more energetic activities, the one thing they could offer to
the rest of the congregation was their support in prayer and
an interior life which could really add richness to everybody else. It was things like that, easily overlooked in a
busy parish, which Terry took very seriously."

Towards the end of 1963 an advertisement appeared in
the Church Army's quarterly. It had been placed on behalf
of the then Bishop of Bristol, the Rt Rev. Oliver Tomkins,
who was looking for someone to organize the training of
lay people in his diocese. In those days Church Army
officers could not apply for posts, they had to be recommended for them. It was an arrangement well suited to
Terry Waite who, as Gordon Kitney has said, was never
ambitious in the worldly sense. "He isn't a career person,
you see. What he does springs from selflessness. He wants
to put the faith he has to the best advantage of the Church,
and to meet some of the needs of a suffering world. It
sounds awfully like a cliché, I know, but it happens to be
true. I remember sitting with Terry in our training days,
listening to a sermon on the Gethsemane experience. It was
a sermon which moved us both very deeply. The simplicity
of it all; Christ going apart from his disciples and saying,

'Father, thy will not mine be done'. It's that which leads Terry on. He's very conscious in everything he does that he is there to do his Father's will."

Once recommended for the new job he was very soon appointed, and so began the latest chapter in his church càreer. The process by which he came to Bristol was a simple one – and one doubtless familiar to all those who have had relatives unjustly imprisoned abroad and sought his help. Terry Waite came to Bristol, to a new challenge which would shape the rest of his life, not so much out of choice but because, quite simply, he was asked.

4

"GIFTED SON OF THE CHURCH"

"When I first met Terry he'd only been married a fortnight, and there we were, about to set off for Geneva together for a two-week course at the Ecumenical Institute!" It is with a mixture of admiration, incredulousness and immense warmth that Canon Laurence Reading – now retired, but in the sixties in charge of adult education for the Anglican Church – remembers his first encounter with the young Church Army captain assigned to the Bristol diocese. "The Institute ran courses and attracted about seventy or eighty church leaders from all over the world. There must have been thirty or forty nationalities represented there, assembled to discuss the whole of Church mission, what its aims were and how best to achieve it among all the different denominations. And in the middle of all this here's old Terry! A mere lad, in a way, and only just married!"

For a couple of years he had been engaged to Helen Frances Watters, the daughter of a Belfast solicitor, whom he had met in the Church Army days. Marriage, according to Gordon Kitney, came as something of a surprise to those with whom he had trained. "Terry and I were both thought of as confirmed bachelors in our College days. We both sort of threw ourselves into our religious vocation, dashing off here and there, and sinking our energies into schemes and projects which many people thought didn't give us time to settle down. But I suppose we all do settle sooner or later, and it was with Frances that he fell in love and with her that he settled down."

And so it was that the newly-wed couple made their way to the West Country to be involved in what people at the time regarded as exciting, pioneering days in the life of the Church. But as Laurence Reading, Terry's mentor and friend, has made clear, hardly had Terry had chance to settle himself down at all to married life than he was on his travels again. Although this time he was off to places with a more exotic ring to them than Cleethorpes or Margate, the promise of such exciting travel abroad did not go to his head. He would, as those who knew him at the time confirm, take everything in his (above average) stride. At first meeting, people were struck by his great charm – a boyish enthusiasm coupled with a startling maturity. Looking back on that first meeting, however, Laurence Reading finds it hard to withhold a note of sheer disbelief at how he managed to pull it off and impress wiser heads than his at the Geneva talks. "He would always walk in where nobody else would go. One of his characteristics was to seize, quite unself-consciously, on some simple point that people maybe had been too intense to notice. Then he would raise it directly with them." Like a child asking the simplest questions of an adult who is then forced to admit he's baffled, Terry Waite brought this quality of directness to all he did. Terry didn't have any foreign languages, but somehow he managed to establish a rapport with people of different countries and cultures. And he would actually get up and speak in this great gathering where there were really some very able, high-powered, and influential people."

Geneva and the Institute were many miles away from the villages and the mission meetings of just a few months earlier, but for Terry Waite it all seemed part of the same unbroken path of church service. More variety, perhaps, boats and planes instead of trek-carts and caravans but still, essentially, the same kind of work with the same ultimate aim in view: conveying the Christian faith to the world; not only making it mean something in one's own life, but enabling it to be of value in other people's. Laurence Reading admits Terry was in no sense an academic, and yet he felt at home among academics as much as among the usual mixture of personalities in any other parish. It was from these early days that a very special relationship, he says, grew up between them. "We got on well from the start. Of course, I was old enough to have been his father at the time", says Canon Reading, and indeed there was something of that paternal relationship present in all their dealings. That, at least, is what one might easily surmise. I myself deduced it when I called on him for recollections of the Bristol days for this book. There was an immense sadness in him as he considered the imagined predicament Terry Waite was currently in. He had hoped, he told me, that Terry would not set out again for the Lebanon, had feared this might simply be too dangerous. And now, faced with his month-long absence from public view, he found it hard and painful to contemplate.

The tenderness which grew up between them sprang as much from their genuine fondness for each other as from the constant professional contact they maintained in all their work. Canon Reading can sympathize with the Waite personality which wanted freedom to move, variety to work in, and no rigid structure to impede the natural talents he has. He himself, as someone responsible for adult education in the church, had his base at Church House in Westminster but, as with the young Church Army captain, he was rarely in one place long enough ever to be considered a desk-bound bureaucrat. Sharing the same task, especially when the ground ahead is uncharted, has a habit of drawing people closer together. It was, perhaps, the closeness of pioneers sharing the excitements and adversities of new challenges and experiences, a feeling of being in (and to some extent in control) at the start which cemented their lifelong friendship. What were these new experiences and challenges?

The whole operation began with the Bishop of Bristol, the Rt Rev. Oliver Tomkins, who was looking for help to get Stewardship and Laity Training (or SALT as it was known) off the ground in his diocese. It is, perhaps, a rather typical piece of ecclesiastical jargon whose rather staid title belies the nature of the endeavour. However staid it appeared, though, Terry Waite was certainly the man to enliven it, as all those who became involved can testify. SALT was an attempt to give depth to the claim that "stewardship" in the scriptural sense was not only about money (whether looking after it or coughing up during the collection) but involved all of a Christian's time and talents. It was an attempt to get lay people, the ordinary folk in a parish, actively involved in the life and work of the Church as a whole. It was vital for the Bishop to appoint a layman to do the job because to have a local vicar at the head of it all would defeat the object. Bishop Tomkins had heard good reports of Captain Terry Waite in York and elsewhere, and was immediately impressed when he interviewed him for the job. Enthusiasm and wisdom are two of the words he has since used when singling out his qualities. But more than that, he says, he LIKED the man. Warmth of personality, the ability to get along with all sorts: had not people all along said these were the key features of the future special envoy? Here, now, was the job that could harness them.

Terry Waite was assigned initially to work with a clergyman, Canon Basil Moss, and between them the

Bishop intended an equal partnership to balance out. "In Basil Moss we already had someone working on the clerical side of the stewardship movement. What we were looking for was someone with sufficient theological expertise to be able to conduct study groups and a programme of education, and yet at the same time someone who, because he didn't wear a dog-collar, could establish a role as one layman talking to another."

Working so closely with the clergy and being so involved in the mainstream activities of church life, it would have been very tempting for many men to consider the ordained ministry as their obvious vocation. But that is something which has never appealed to Terry Waite, even from the earliest days. As he has on more than one occasion said, becoming a priest would have involved him, quite rightly, following a clearly defined path. He would have been given to a particular congregation and would have had to commit all his time and efforts to the demands of one locality. On the positive side it would have given him a sense of permanence in a place and a degree of security. But that approach has never been his, he has said, and turning his back on it has involved a degree of risk. Never quite knowing which job he will be doing next – or if, indeed, there is a job there to go to at all – has meant paying a price in vulnerability, isolation and the nervousness of not knowing "what next", but despite it all he prefers the freelance path he has taken. It would be a mistake to see the twists and turns of an unpredictable career as evidence of a buccaneering irresponsibility (though his friends also point out that there is more than a shade of the adventurer in his make-up), when he himself has always said that such calculated uncertainty is a genuine part of his Christian vocation. For now his work is well within the Church's mainstream. In future times, he has said, who knows

whether that Christian vocation will *keep* him in the
Church. And such was the whole aim of the SALT years –
that whether in or out of the Church people should be
encouraged to put their faith into effect. That was the
theory, but, as many clergymen in Bristol at the time knew
from first-hand experience, putting it into practice was a
hard job. That was where Terry Waite came in.

The parish of Ashton Gate in Bedminster had some six
thousand people in it at the time, and John Wilson was its
priest. "This part of Bristol was a very densely populated
area, and one which was completely dominated by the
Wills Cigarette and Cigar factory. That's where most of the
work was. Now it so happened that the majority of those
attending the church were employed at the factory but in
their day-to-day lives didn't carry a great deal of responsibility at work, which meant that they were reluctant
to assume any in the church. Having a say in things wasn't
part of their experience, so they'd no reason to believe they
could be in charge of anything anywhere – least of all in the
church, where the vicar ran the show. And that's where
Terry's help was important. He played a part in encouraging ordinary people to see that ministry was not just
the priestly ministry but the ministry of the whole body of
Christ." The realization was not new. Putting it into effect
was in some people's minds nothing short of revolutionary
because people's attitudes had already been moulded.

John Wilson continued: "I don't think he necessarily ran
courses in 'How to be a Church warden' or 'How to
become a member of the church council', he just came
along and talked to people. And, believe me, that was new
in those days. He would meet different groups and
persuade them that they did have the potential if only they
could unlock it. In those days we were beginning to understand the importance of meeting in small groups outside

Sunday worship, to study the Bible, for example, or to give
attention to some of the moral and religious issues of the
day. It may not have been true of other parishes but it was
certainly true of areas like mine that there were very few
people, if any, who would want or feel competent to lead
new schemes. I remember with dismay, I think after Terry's
initial visit, that a particular scheme had been suggested.
The idea was for the congregation itself to take the initiative but at the council meeting they told me, 'Oh, it
would be so much easier if you got on with it, vicar. You're
trained to do this sort of thing.' But as a result of Terry
coming along and encouraging folk to lead groups themselves, people gradually began to have a role to play. And
alongside that, of course, it was helping them to see the
relevance of the Gospel message in their everyday lives. To
give you a current example. We have a young couple in the
parish where I am now who are not regular church
attenders but they've started because they're about to get
married here. Now it so happened that one of my curates
had preached a sermon on social action and social concern,
basing it on the prophet Amos. It was only when they'd
heard it that they suddenly realized there was actually a
connection between what you hear in church on Sunday
and what happens in the world outside during the rest of
the week. Now transplant that into our parish of twenty-
odd years ago and you've got a perfect example of the kind
of attitudes Terry was dealing with at the time. He would
tell them that the church isn't simply a ghetto for people
who are 'that way inclined' to meet every now and again,
but that it's the salt (to use the term of the time) to add
flavour to the whole of life outside it."

The success of work of this kind is hard to gauge, but
those who were at the receiving end of it insist that the
quality of parish life increased immeasurably after Terry

Waite had passed through. And he left his personal stamp on things, too, exploding on the scene with schemes, ideas and plans while much later the fall-out from his own personality worked its encouraging effects.

To give but one illustration. We had travelled half a mile in John Wilson's car before he realized that he had set off through the streets of Clifton after dark without switching his headlights on. There was more inattention to come when a couple of miles further on we sailed (at a sedate pace and within a tolerable margin of risk) through red lights at a crossroads. "I don't normally do this sort of thing", he said to me. "It's just that I do enjoy talking about Terry and the work he did. Such a likeable, big-hearted man." I had travelled down to Bristol to get first-hand accounts from friends and colleagues, and thought it wise to continue the interview with John Wilson somewhere other than in a moving vehicle. Horfield Rectory, his own base at the other side of Bristol, seemed safer.

"When I came to the Bedminster diocese I was really rather disheartened by what I saw, but then Terry appeared, if you like, as a gift from God! I remember how he cut an attractive figure in our area, and one of the church council saying what a delightful man we had here, hoping he'd be coming back again. It's often the case that prophets are without honour in their own country, and in some ways it was like that with the clergy. People wouldn't necessarily take from a parish priest what they'd take from Terry."

And it is here that another of the man's qualities, as much apparent in world affairs as domestic parish matters, becomes obvious – his independence. The word suggests at times, however, a certain distance from the organization one serves. In Terry Waite's case, the word needs further

61

clarification. As the Archbishop of Canterbury's envoy in Libya and Lebanon he maintained his independence of national politics. As a lay training officer in Bristol he may have been independent of church hierarchy but he was definitely welded to the institution itself. Elizabeth Ralph, a historian and retired city archivist, was a prominent figure in lay church circles at the time, and expresses it as follows. "He was the model lay Christian with a vocation which was undeniable. He isn't one of these 'freelance Christians' who don't want anything to do with the institutional Church. He has never despised the institution and never worked outside it. He may have spotted some of its weaknesses and done his bit (more than his bit) to correct them, but he's been perfectly happy working right at the heart of it. You don't join the Church Army, I suppose, if you want to work outside it. And then again, years later, when he went to work for the Roman Catholics in Rome, he was very much part of a highly structured institution but, as an Anglican, retaining that certain degree of distance or room to manoeuvre. Nevertheless he served within that structure, and I'd never describe him as a freelance, roving iconoclastic person at all."

His arrival in Bristol was initially viewed with reserve. As one (by preference anonymous) source told me, "You see, you had a slot for Church Army people who were just commissioned and had been allotted to your parish. They came along in their uniform with a known tradition behind them, and although I personally valued them very highly in certain areas of work, the idea of having one as your sidekick was sometimes hard to swallow. The average Church Army officer was rather wet, rather evangelical, a bit heavy-handed and it was hard for me not to get rather impatient with the way they could operate. I respect the movement very much, but in the average parochial system the list of preferences went as follows: If you have to have someone attached to you and you can't have a curate, well, you might as well have a deaconess. And if you can't have a deaconess, well, you'll have to put up with a Church Army captain! They were associated with seaside missions, pamphlets, and banners and that sort of thing. Well, frankly that's not my style. But on the occasions I met Terry I have to say he completely shattered that image."

So Terry Waite arrived somewhat as an unknown quantity, with a reputation preceding him which led some to expect great things and others to fear the worst. Within a short space of time he had endeared himself to all.

On one fine spring morning Elisabeth Ralph received an invitation. It was an offer she would have liked to refuse but could not. It came from the Bishop, who was asking her if she would chair a committee to set up the formal agenda for laity training in the diocese. She arrived at the spot designated for the weekend deliberations – a country retreat in Shipham not far from the picture postcard beauty of the Cheddar Gorge – and took a quiet intake of breath. A scholarly and impressive woman herself she was, none the less, unprepared for what she saw. A Methodist minister, a lawyer, a monk from Downside, and a Professor of Veterinary Surgery – and, of course, the looming figure of Terry Waite, all lined up and waiting for the chairman to arrive. They could have been the distinguished house guests for an Agatha Christie weekend thriller for all Miss Ralph knew, and she immediately felt overwhelmed by the task. But Terry himself offered his own brand of encouragement and she agreed to take on the chairmanship. He had had a hand in setting up the agenda and so was able to keep a discreet eye on proceedings. He took his seat on the committee with only one piece of advice to the nervous chairman, "Make sure we're all through by 9.30

and we can all go off to the local" – minor but invaluable advice guaranteed to oil the wheels of social relationships, and to generate the kind of harmony which would give their new venture the much-needed initial push.

Residential courses, weekend seminars, training pro-grammes held in all sorts of changing locations now be-came the staple fare of the newly appointed lay training officer, and he took to it all with enormous appetite. The aim was not to stand out at the front with pointer and projector and to talk to the audience, the aim was to allow everyone to take an active part. It meant – the phrase crops up yet again – "getting on with people", learning how others tick. By this time Terry was in his element and enjoying the experience. His colleague, Laurence Reading, who frequently accompanied him on the courses, noticed how he was polishing up his already winning ways. "I remember that one place where we got a group of people together had this great dragon of a proprietress. He would jolly her along and tease her in a way no one of us would dare do and she loved it all. She also had a bit of a temper and could be very awkward if she chose to, but old Terry would cope marvellously with that charm of his. He'd go and sort things out in the nicest possible way and, lo and behold, all would be smiles again and we would all sigh with relief. He was very good at disarming awkward people, and especially good at persuading chaps who didn't really want to get involved."

The textbook example of this quality, the lesson number one, if you will, in any intermediary study of Terry Waite's persuasive powers is provided by the circumstances of the Bristol Diocesan Clergy Conference which took place one fine summer in the middle sixties. It was to be held that year at Butlin's Holiday Camp, Minehead. "Oh dear", thought some members of the clergy, unfamiliar with the distinctive attractions of this traditionally English high-season venue. "I think, by and large," says John Wilson, "they were rather reluctant to go to Butlin's, whether it was Minehead or anywhere else, and I think the Bishop, Oliver Tomkins, was aware of it. Now, he was a very wise man indeed and he wrote a splendid letter to everybody concerned. 'At the time of your ordination,' he wrote, 'you promised to obey your Bishop in all things lawful and honest. I cannot see anything unlawful in my requiring you to come to Butlin's Holiday Camp this time.' So we all had a three-line whip on this, and there was no getting out of it. But this is where Terry came in. He was there more as an observer really but entered into it all in a way which made it irresistible. Frances had had twins, in the first year of their settling in Bristol, and by now Ruth and Clare were toddlers. He took the family along, and I can see him now leaping into Butlin's swimming pool and making an effort to ensure the atmosphere was relaxed for everyone. I can remember my wife and I were rather alarmed at first to see him splashing about with a young child under each arm, but jumping in like that was somehow just the right thing to do. It was almost as if by climbing into the pool himself he could put everybody at their ease and encourage them to do the same. It was a case of entering into the spirit of things – literally and figuratively!"

To some people the week-long clergy summer school at Minehead may only have been memorable for the 'flu virus which did the rounds and made inroads into the concentration levels of the participants, but by others, like John Wilson, it will be remembered as a time when Terry Waite's own brand of infectious personality had its traditional, salutary effect on all who came into contact with that "beaming smile which radiated warmth, joy and concern". And they got some work done into the bargain.

The whole emphasis on training and ministry was going through great changes, and Terry's arrival and talents coincided neatly with the new approach. The idea of "specialist" ministry, according to John Wilson, had undergone profound change. It used to be thought that people came in with these "specialist", somehow magical, skills which they then worked on the people in the parish. There was a slightly pejorative undertone to it as well, he says, implying as it did a kind of mysterious outsider brought in to sort everybody out. Terry Waite, he adds, would have resisted that title very fiercely. In one sense it was a very specialized ministry he was engaged in but in another it was very straightforward and obvious, drawing, as it did, not on some academic theory or acquired skill for its effect, but on the very qualities, talents, and strengths of the people at the receiving end. In other words the ordinary people in the parish were not being *told* to form their study groups or *told* to organize themselves, they were being encouraged, enabled to do it all for themselves. No specialist ministry, this. But by common consent Terry Waite was always rather special himself.

The quality Oliver Tomkins had noticed and valued was that of empathy with different kinds of lay people. Acting, even then, as a mediator between them and the clergy was a key task. As someone organizing groups and conferences, and travelling around to persuade clergy and lay people to give up their time to go on training programmes, he was given a job only the genuinely dedicated could perform. The aim – to equip ordinary people to be articulate and well-informed leaders of local Christian communities – was simple enough on paper, as was encouraging them to see the relevance of their Christian faith in everyday life. But to make the ideals part of the very fabric of parish life needed someone who could not only communicate with people but associate with them, too. As a layman himself Terry Waite was well placed to do both. His tolerance and his firmness of purpose endeared him to the Bishop. He was, quite simply, "the man for the job" – a keen Christian who did not see the need to be ordained to achieve the Church's aims. Older heads think twice before praising wisdom and judgement in their juniors, but Oliver Tomkins had no hesitation in commending them in a man "who knew where he wanted to go but didn't bulldoze anyone in the process, who had the endless capacity to draw out from silent people, from shy people, the gifts which often they themselves did not know they had."

What natural gifts Terry Waite had in those Bristol days were assisted by new techniques which had their origins across the Atlantic. He acquired them for himself and became an accomplished exponent in what, in the jargon of the time, were known as "group dynamics" or "T-groups". These "T" or training groups took many by surprise. This was the procedure.

A course was arranged for the clergy by Terry. It would be a week-long affair, and old hands at this sort of thing would know what to expect from this typical brand of residential course, with its lectures, talks and set agenda. At least, they would *think* they knew what to expect. All of them would be in for a very big surprise. Day one and the clergy troop in like innocent lambs. Terry sits at the front in silence. The clergy are silent. There is more silence. A few coughs punctuate the quiet but no one speaks. More silence. But wait a minute, isn't Terry supposed to be organizing this thing? Why is he not saying anything? Terry sits back quite relaxed, surveys the room but says nothing. This terrible silence cannot continue. Someone speaks. 'When are we starting, then?" Terry replies, "Whenever you like." Silence. "Oh, this is all a waste of time", says one. "Look, I've got a busy parish to run back in Bristol. I haven't got time for all this nonsense", says another. Gradually a conversation (not always amicable) breaks out, and raises questions from the floor of the kind that would normally be on the agenda. The participants are setting their own agenda and working out in a quite muscular way what it is that really is of importance to them.

The process of orchestrating the "dynamics" of the group took time and did not suit everyone. It was generally thought that the presence of the Rt Rev. C. L. P. Bishop (or "Jim" to his familiars) in the actual training session would inhibit the free exchange of opinion, so he kept very much in the background, exercising, as he put it, "a calming influence at meal-times and so on, when the priests would come out exasperated by the whole enterprise". The gradual movement from annoyance to acceptance followed a fairly constant course. By Tuesday of the week's course people were "seething, fed up with the lot", and some might even have packed their bags and gone. But by Wednesday morning the mood would have changed and all would suddenly become animated, talking freely and excited at the prospect of, for once, being able to speak their minds. By Friday they would be converts to the technique, all swearing it was a marvellous experience they would love to repeat. Terry was the heart of it, yet they had done all the work.

His role in all this was that of the observer and the gentle "prodder" giving the discussion a nudge here, a bit of fine tuning there, and in the end re-telling to the participants what they had heard, how exactly it had been said, and by whom. If, for example, a dominant voice emerged to which everyone was suddenly assenting, he would point it out. If an insistent voice was making it difficult for opposition to be heard, he explained the phenomenon. And if a knot of people was content to say nothing and go along with everything, then that, too, was announced to all. The end result was that people began to realize how decisions actually do get made, and how lay people might feel when they found themselves in similar situations in parish meetings. How easy it was for the shy to say nothing and for the loudest voices to carry the day. How easy it was to disagree with what was going on but be powerless to influence events. This was the core of the T-groups. And it had enormous practical side effects.

Canon Raymond Harris, twenty-eight years a priest in Swindon, remembers the impact vividly. "These were totally unstructured groups so that what did emerge was a structure all the more durable for not being artificially structured in the first place. And you could relate what happened there to what regularly happened, say, at your church council meetings. Most clergy, if they were honest, would admit they hogged the show. In worship and study, too, the same thing happened. The parson preached the sermon and left it at that, handing out a spoonful of medicine, as it were, instead of asking the congregation to take a hand in its own well-being. Let's say you had an important matter to discuss with your parish at an AGM. Perhaps you were wanting to alter the form of worship, or organize a youth club, or let young people use your immaculate church hall for rehearsing a play. Whatever it might be, by and large, the clergy ruled the roost. The vicar would surround himself with a small army of yes-men, prime up the undecided, and, by drawing up the agenda and the terms of the discussion, make jolly sure he got what he wanted."

They are observations familiar to many a parish priest – certainly to Jim Bishop. "How many times did you hear post-mortems after the PCC meeting, with people who'd stayed silent all the while mumbling that they hadn't got what they wanted?" The new style that Terry Waite and others were pioneering exploded the myth of democratic decision-making, and revealed conclusively that inside many a soi-disant liberal-minded parson was a Great Dictator who had rigged the ballot. The effect was bracing. From now on they were encouraged to use the chair as a position from which to offer service to the parish, not to rule it; to encourage the shy and keep a control over the garrulous, the domineering, and, yes, the boring. The sessions could be very heavy, as Raymond Harris has particular reason to recall. "My brother-in-law, also a priest, was at one of these sessions. Now he is a very quiet, reserved type of person. After some minutes of the preliminary silence and a few sporadic bursts of discontent one vicar stood up and gestured towards him with the words, 'Well, come on, why don't you help us out? You've been quiet all this time, why don't you say something?' At which point my brother-in-law, normally quite a timid sort said, 'I'm not saying much because for the moment I've got nothing to say. But I will say one thing. You're getting on my nerves!' So these sessions were very revealing of an underlying 'aggro' in all of us. There were lighter moments at the pub, but during the working period it could get quite intense. Then Terry would have to step in quietly. On a number of occasions people were all ready to leave, and once again Terry would discreetly intervene and explain it all one-to-one."

The whole process was revealing of the character of the clergy, and threw into sharp focus the attitudes they in turn presented to their flock. Whereas the young, inexperienced vicar might feel the need to go into his new parish and show who was in control, he now learnt to withdraw a little from events and let decisions emerge. Whereas he might feel the need to heal all divisions with a soothing word, he now learnt that in some cases it could be wiser to open up the wound, clean it out and let it fully heal over. Certainly Jim Bishop marvelled at what Terry was achieving, and regretted that he, as a young clergyman, had never had the benefit of this approach. "If only I'd known in my PCC meetings of long ago what I was beginning to learn then," he says wistfully, "I'd have missed out on so much unpleasantness, so many misunderstandings."

What the clergy was being asked to decide was whether Christian service or empire building was really at the heart of its ministry. "I'm going to have to give you a bit of a sermon here", says Raymond Harris. "Hold on tight! If we truly believe that God accepts us as we are, and that we belong to Him as children, then we have to express that joyful brotherhood in our lives. When someone new walks into our church, for example, we and the whole church have to convey our concern for the newcomer not try to keep him at arm's length. Unwittingly, by our attitudes so many of us did (and do) just that. These courses in, for want of a better word, 'self awareness' helped us to understand the barriers the clergy itself were putting up. I mean, I can remember spending two hours discussing whether to issue the cleaner with a short, nine-inch broom, or a foot-long one. Two hours! And why was that? The answer is that up until that point they'd never had any idea how decisions were made. If a fête was to be organized they were *told* a fête was to be organized, if a mission was to be held a mission *was* held and they did what the vicar said. But with a nine-inch broom, well, they knew a thing or two about that, so they got in there and started to get excited. Now they could really influence events! So the whole point was to cash in on that and make their contribution count for something in parish life."

While Terry Waite was organizing countless numbers of these training groups he was also doing his best to keep up with a busy family life. Doing at least two things at once was something at which he became decidedly adept. Oliver Tomkins, for instance, remembers going round to the Waite home to see Terry bathing the twins with one hand and reading Kafka with the other. "Do get across his humour," I was told by those who have known him, "his quick repartee, his love of good fun and jokes. Tell them how good he is with children." Certainly he was good with Jim Bishop's family, and on two very different occasions which revealed two aspects of his sensitive gifts. The first, says Jim Bishop, was nothing particular really, "It was just one summer's day in Bristol when he was watching my young son splash around in his tiny paddling pool in the garden. The next thing I knew, off came his shoes and socks and he was in there with him to the wild excitement of my little boy. But then much later, when he was about twelve or thirteen, he'd got into a bit of trouble, and I remember pouring it all out to Terry, and he said in that immensely reassuring way, 'Don't worry, it's only a phase. All children go through it.' And just to be comforted in that way by so young a man was something I've never for-gotten."

Years later Terry was to buy a caravan and keep it parked among the gorse bushes in Jim's garden in Cley, in Norfolk, where he has now retired. There were trips in the car to the beaches, long walks with the children. Once Terry had bought a job lot of bicycles at an auction and spent the day repairing them for the children before an outing was arranged. And it was during one of these

carefree country holidays in 1980 that the first word of
trouble in Iran reached Terry Waite from Lambeth Palace.
By the next morning the Archbishop's envoy was gone.

He enjoyed his work and was respected for it. The
Bristol clergy loved him and felt no sense of jealousy or
intrusion. Oliver Tomkins recognized that his status as
layman would put him in no danger of posing any threats.
One of their own number could be viewed with more
suspicion, and could be liable to be thought of as butting in
on somebody else's patch. Another vicar coming along to
teach them how to do their jobs would have been a recipe
for conflict. A layman coming into a parish to talk of
liberating the potential of the laity – now that was a
different matter. Here was a person with whom
co-operation was possible without any feeling of in-
security.

It was in Bristol, in the midst of professional (and
pastoral) success and a happy family life that a major
sadness in his life occurred. His father had been diagnosed
as having lung cancer and, as Terry's brother, David, remembers, had been given six months to live. "The six
months came and went and turned eventually into eighteen
months. For me, and I'm sure for Terry, every day that did
come would see me asking myself if it would be today that
my father would die. Terry would make regular trips up
from Bristol to see his dad, and in those last months they
got very close to each other, which both of them
appreciated. I would say it was a tremendous comfort to
my father. I was the one who, in a sense, didn't know how
to handle things, whereas he was far more able to cope
with it. It was an emotional time for us all, but all the time
Terry would keep that emotion inside rather than show his
grief openly. I remember him taking the funeral, or part of
it at least, which he did in a very professional, very

sensitive way." In the timing of his father's death there was a particular sadness which affected Terry, then aged twenty-eight, very deeply. He came up to the family home at weekends to see his father, but one weekend he telephoned to say he was due to preach in Bristol. Would it be all right if he didn't come? His mother assured him that his father's condition had not changed, and told him to go ahead with the preaching date. She takes up the story. "It was that very night he died and Terry couldn't come. It upset him an awful lot. I rang him up and he was here by midnight, very, very sad that he had not been able to be there."

In private prayer and public worship it was clear to everyone that Terry Waite was a very devout man. It was not the authority of Holy Orders which he generated, but that which sprang from his natural talents and from his spiritual application. As Elizabeth Ralph puts it, "You feel that Terry carries an inner authority, one not bestowed on him by earthly powers or even by the Church, but directly by God Himself. I remember saying to Bishop Oliver once that he really does seem to be a man whom God is using."

Back in Bristol the Bishop himself had particular reason to value this divine instrument. "This whole SALT business was very much part of the wider Stewardship Movement of the Church of England of the time, and he could very easily have presented it as a money-raising gimmick for a Church which was finding diminishing resources rather painful. We wanted very much to get away from the money side of things and develop the awareness of the Church as being primarily the laity committed to giving *all* their gifts. But rather ironically one practical illustration I remember did indeed revolve around cash. When I arrived in the diocese the average stipend was £650 a year, and we decided it was not good enough, so I appointed a commission of lay people to look at this and to report back what they felt was a just figure. After some deliberation they came to the conclusion that £1,000 should be the recommended figure. We took a deep breath and said it was really impossible for anyone to raise that amount of money in the diocese. However, it was in that context of asking the lay people of the parishes to be the ones to bear the burden of clerical stipends that the first idea of the laity's full participation began." It was Terry Waite who was formally to have the first job of pioneering that participation. One of his strengths was to know when he had done enough to be able to let go, to know where he would find fruitful results and then to leave them to get on with it so that he could go elsewhere to where resistances were greater.

People often refer to a certain boyishness in Terry Waite the man. Laurence Reading takes it further. "It's a kind of childlike quality, really, which somehow gets directly to another person. It's an almost Franciscan attitude he brings to things. This chap really does believe, you know. And he's got it right. He isn't an evangelist in the strict sense, nor a proselytizer; he just embodies the faith, letting it infuse all he does."

During his time in Bristol, when Terry Waite travelled widely at home and abroad, he was chosen as part of an international team from England, America and Africa to conduct training courses for the bishops and senior clergy of Uganda. His great strengths of mastering the art and the craft of the psychological T-group methods, coupled with his natural ability to humanize the whole process and to keep himself from being carried away by the jargon of it all, impressed themselves on everyone.

"The ideal would be to leave in every parish an inner group of committed lay people who knew each other, trusted each other and were committed to dedicating to the service of God whatever gifts they had." Oliver Tomkins, who hired Terry Waite in the first place to implement that idea in Bristol, sketches out here a blueprint for a developing church, and it was just such a blueprint which appealed to the church in Uganda when in 1969 it hired Terry Waite for a three-year term as a lay trainer to serve its growing needs. Characteristically he accepted the new challenge, and with wife and family set off for Africa and for fresh adventures.

So what of lasting value did he achieve in his first job in Bristol? Canon Raymond Harris, still working in the area, is ideally placed to assess the impact twenty years on. "The real changes he brought about were in people's ways of thinking. Anybody can make superficial changes and think they've achieved a lot. It doesn't take much real talent to build an annexe to the church, to inaugurate a new meeting hall or to rearrange the seating. But to alter the time-hallowed ways in which people behave and allow them to see ahead with a clearer vision, now, that, to my mind, is real and lasting achievement we can all be proud of."

1a Training for the Church Army, 1958

1b Terry in his early 20s – Gordon Kitney walks directly ahead

2a The young lay training officer, in Bristol

3 *(Opposite)* With Desmond Tutu, at a press conference in Downing Street, London, 1985

2b Entebbe, Uganda, 1971

2

4 (*Opposite*)
In Cape Town, Terry comforts refugee children sheltering in a church. They had been ordered to leave a white area

5a Terry telephoning in the Lebanon

6 - 7 (*Overleaf*)
The world – and the press – reacting to news of Terry

5b In London with the Archbishop of Canterbury

Cool Waite takes shower as bullets fly in deadly gun battle

Waite taking cover yesterday

ICE-COOL Terry Waite missed death by inches yesterday when a bullet smashed into the wall of a flat in Beirut at the height of a gun battle.

Automatic fire ra..........
below, rocket............
htudded...............
W......................

Express Foreign Service

the be........ rival Moslem
.... England envoy.
.... floor office of
.... ly otld jour-
.... oyed by hte
.... ency: "I'm

PERSONALITY OF THE WEEK

An envoy of rare talents

CAUGHT in the stutter of crossfire in Beirut and holed up out of sight, Terry Waite dodged the bullets but not the question.

"What are you going to do now?" yelled a newsman. "Take cover, I think," he shouted back.

Waite was in the thick of one of his most dangerous missions — to secure the safe release of four American hostages. Ironically, his personal safety was something he could joke about.

For all his efforts to play down his idiosyncratic form of shuttle diplomacy, Waite (45) has become a hero and could well ever aspire to be.

The Archbishop of Canterbury's special envoy is one of churchmen.

Humour is one of the secrets of his success. "He has a tremendous energy of you put him in a room with any group of people, however impossible, they will begin working together."

His size — he is 6ft over 2in — is another asset. "Very different people defer to him, and he is so tall. He has a natural authority. That and his directness and humour is a combination," says a Lambeth palace colleague.

His style and negotiation has a warmth and frankness about it which contrasts sharply with the subtler ways of listening class and diplomatic. He is a good listener, yet can focus attention on the human being involved in a dispute, and with his impressive size and manner inspires trust, and he carries himself fairly among people with different views from himself.

He argues, for instance, that Colonel Gaddafi of Libya should not be written off and that he was once attacked by an American journalist. "Colonel Gaddafi are some of the face to face, and you'd think of him as a genial manner and it wasn't only this sense of a man that measured times of a man of faith that measured through to a Lib yan leader, with whom he established a good rapport.

He has an astute brain, a powerful grasp of foreign policy and philosophy and that before cunning can make him a first class negotiator. Even his first clash with Henry Kissinger.

He thinks on his feet. He had not reached Tripoli before his meeting with Gaddafi in his major stumbling the major harassment in the

thought up on the spot," he says.

Yet the preparations for his visit left nothing to chance. Months of patient work preceded it and he did not go until the signs were favourable.

He was a diplomat's a coolness in a cri sis but maintained a temper. He lost it when he reached the airport with the picture hostages four years ago and was told an eleventh-hour delay.

The people who knew him while keeping a bishop's "exposed distance from the arch bishop's public platform is privately) passionate about his talents. It would have liked to use him to serve his country had he not already decided to serve his God.

Terry Waite grew up in Styal, Che shire. of a village policeman. As a boy, he dreamed of travel. He joined the Grenadier Guards but had to leave be cause he found himself allergic to the khaki dye.

Then studied theology at the Church Army College but because he was attracted by the London and the United States. Later he moved to Rome.

He worked on the Anglican Church in Britain before becoming an adviser to the first African Archbishop of the Province of Uganda, Erica Sabiti.

For an he worked for the Roman Cath olic Church as a consultant on African work in Africa and then for the arrival at Lambeth. Shortly after Dr Runcie latest-ago Lambeth, showed his small African sec retary for Anglican communion affairs.

The last four Christmases have involved real sacrifice. He is a devoted family man, telephoning them regularly from distant parts of the world.

Frances. A Belfast solicitor daughter is in... with her at-ease as real is comfortable in the spotlight with a 19-year-old, 20-year-old twin-four children. daughter and his son, 18-year-old. They live in a terraced son. They live in a terraced house servant's of the old located in the at the Travellers the likes more reads the Travellers the likes more reads society. He is on work one, bicycle often has to work one. bicycle

He may say sometimes fall in real but, especially in won efforts nearer freed, he will still properly nearer freed. The everybody she is Maybe nobody else to yet ventured to complain with in meddling in so

Joy of freedom

AMERICAN hostage David Jacobsen shared his first day of freedom yesterday with the man who made it possible — Britain's Terry Waite.

Months of captivity for Mr Jacobsen mused on his 17 and said: "I am very, very happy. The best things in life are free."

Giving special thanks to Mr Waite, 55-year-old Jacobsen said: "Terry is a man of hope.

"Our darkest hour was in September 1985 when we heard he was leaving West Beirut. But in that sadness he gave us some thing we needed—he gave us hope. Even then we felt he had not let us down. We love this guy."

We love Waite, says hostage on way home

From JOHN ENGLAND in Wiesbaden

When the two men arrived at the American base at Wiesbaden in a private jet, Servicemen and their families applauded.

They unfurled a banner saying: "Welcome home, Mr Jacobsen."

The former hostage said: "I want to cry. My Danish parents will be

happy to see my name spelled right."

He was near tears when he spoke of his fellow hostages still in captivity.

"I have mixed feelings to be a free man again.

Hell

"We pray to God that they will soon be released. Those guys are in hell. We have got to get them out."

Then referring to the video which showed him

criticising the American administration for forget ting the hostages, Mr Jacobsen said: "I want right now to thank the American President and the United States and all the civil servants who worked on this.

"We live in the world's greatest democracy. I am proud to be an American"

Hopes are still high that Mr Waite may still be able to gain freedom for other American, French and British hostages.

Where is Waite?

Mystery over t... to free Ameri...

THE whereabouts of Terry Waite, missing for 72 hours on his most perilous hostage mission yet, were shrouded in mystery yesterday.

Some reports in the Lebanese capital Beirut said the Archbishop of Canterbury's special envoy had been kidnapped.

These were later denied, with assurances that Mr Waite was negotiating with fanatical Muslim gunmen for the release of American Terry Anderson, journalists, and academic Thomas Sutherland.

Rumours

Amid the confusion, Mr Waite's wife Frances was said to be deeply upset and concerned for his safety after seeing a TV-am report of his 'kidnap'. The story was later retracted.

It is believed that Mr Waite, who has said in the past that he risks becoming a hostage himself during his tense negotiations with the Lebanese gunmen, vanished from his hotel on Tuesday. He had been under the protection of the Druze Muslim warlord Walid Jumblatt.

Druze militia said yesterday that the kidnap rumours were spread by 'suspect radio stations.'

A spokesman said: 'Waite is all right and we believed guarantees.' He refused to give details, but added : 'Waite is not in danger. He is continuing his mission.'

Many people in Beirut expect Mr Waite to surface today.

From ...

A Christian ... of Lebanon, a... Syrian-controll ... Lebanon, and ... Iranian Hezbo... the release o...

In London ... man John M... no reason to ... well, continu ...

They hi... personally ... 'Terry ... moment ... this. He h... be ever hi... be secur ... He woul ... Jumblat ...

La... Keatl... repor... later ... very ...

tim ... Wa ... am ... in ... ad ... be ...

WAITE IS KIDNAP HOSTAGE

By JOHN DICKIE, Diplomatic Correspondent

ENVOY Terry Waite has b... kidnapped, it was reported Beirut last night.

The 47-year-old mediator sent by the A... bishop of Canterbury to negotiate the re... of Western hostages held by Shi'ite extrem... was said to have been tricked into becomi... hostage himself.

A Moslem militia official qu... Reuter's newsagency in the ... capital claimed he had bee... against his will since he disa... from his hotel 11 days ago.

... Waite dispensed with his... had believed he was being ... ... alks with the abd... ... victim of a ... ... seized ... ... rele...

Terror group 'find Briton guil...

THE TRIAL OF TERRY WAITE

Waite: Trapped

JOHN HAMSHIRE in Larnaca, Cyprus

RY WAITE could be ... a death ... eing put sen...

8a Terry at Lambeth Palace, London, with released American hostages David Jacobsen, the Rev. Lawrence Jenco and the Rev. Ben Weir

8b Shortly before his disappearance, Terry relaxes – while his Druse guards keep watch

5

PLACE OF PEACE

The Rev. P. Turner, Chairman of the Uganda Lay Training Board, stared in horror and disbelief at the front page of *The Uganda Argus*. Terry Waite, recently hired to head the new training programme, was due to arrive in Kampala at any time. Philip Turner, who would be there to welcome him and show him the ropes, was expecting him that very day. What he was not expecting, when he idly reached for his newspaper that morning, was a front-page news photograph of Terry Waite holding two smaller men by the scruff of the neck. "Oh, my goodness!" he thought, "What have we let ourselves in for?" and buried his face in his hands, half in panic, half in shame. He remembers the incident vividly.

"I took one look at the photograph and couldn't believe my eyes. Here was this huge, great white man collaring these two guys like some great colonialist arriving in foreign parts to take charge. If this was how we were going to start out, what hope did we have for success in the mission work? I was aghast." He rapidly gained his composure when he read on. The caption explained the confusion. Within a few hours of arrival, so the story ran, Terry Waite had intervened in a hold-up and prevented two men from stealing a car. The paper was billing him as a hero, as the strong man fearlessly stepping in to maintain law and order and bringing the criminals to book. Philip Turner was relieved. "How it all happened I still haven't discovered. I mean, I got to know later on that Terry was

always the sort of person to get right in the middle of
things, but to get himself on the front page of the paper
within twenty-four hours, well, that was really
something." Terry Waite had arrived.

In many ways, though, the story is misleading. It can
suggest a man constantly eager for the limelight and
someone who puts publicity of the task above the task
itself. Clearly the man could not have engineered his first
dramatic prominence in the *Uganda Argus*, but it is typical
that his own actions, spontaneous, direct, and sometimes,
say his friends, impetuous, do have a habit of making him a
newsworthy figure. He is not easily defined, not easily
compartmentalized. His taste for the daring is not something he has self-consciously acquired, it is a quality which
those who know him say springs entirely naturally from his
decisive temperament.

Once the first flash of publicity had exploded and
people's eyes had grown accustomed once more to the
natural light, it was time to settle into the job at hand,
which was to help revitalize the Church in Uganda at this
crucial period in its history.

It was during his Bristol years that Terry Waite had
attended a conference in Uganda with a shared aim of
developing leadership and organization within the Church.
Philip Turner, who was then in charge of the work, first
met him during that conference and was greatly impressed,
"I liked him immediately and in fact I pushed hard to get
him to come out here permanently. We actually met in the
Mulago Hospital, where a friend of mine had come down
with appendicitis. As we walked through the ward I was
straightaway taken by his directness. I had him marked
down as a very canny man who would have no trouble in
working with all sorts of different people."

The conference lasted only a couple of weeks, and after

Terry Waite had left to return to England Philip Turner began to shift his attention to the possibility of full-time, permanent work of this type equipped with a roving group of specialist training staff. At the time they had been given a sizeable grant by the Episcopal Church in the United States to start up work of this kind, but the problem was, who to find to take charge of it. As Philip Turner explains, there was an obvious choice. "A lot of people thought at the time that because it was American money we should have an American to head it up. Fortunately, we couldn't find one, and I kept putting Terry's name forward. After a while all parties agreed to the idea, Terry was hired, and that's how he came to be out here for three years."

The training programme to teach both lay people and clergy was not an exclusively Anglican operation, and even from the start it was hoped to work amicably with the Roman Catholic missions and societies, who themselves were anxious to see a developing church grow and thrive. This particular brand of understated ecumenism owed much to Terry Waite himself. "He took to the job immediately and had a wide vision of what it should entail. From the outset he knew it needed to involve the Roman Catholics," says Philip Turner, "and he knew, too, that it should have official backing." It was from that moment on that Terry Waite established a wide range of personal and professional contacts united by their common aim of building up the Church. There had been a long-standing history of division between the Church of Uganda and the Roman Catholic Church, and it was generally felt at the time that if there was to be real and lasting progress fences needed to be mended and co-operation re-established. And that was where the Waite touch came in useful, as he was careful to build Roman Catholics into the programme from the very start. But there was an added reason why the two churches should work together, since they were the only two bodies in the country which really had anything like an organizational structure stretching into practically every village in the land.

"The Million Shilling Syndrome" was how Terry Waite and Philip Turner referred to the phenomenon they discovered in many a community they visited. It was the feeling that when the villagers had a problem they all relied on an outsider to solve it. And that outsider would invariably bring lots of money, bags of shiny shillings, to make the problem go away. Life was not going to be as simple as that, and persuading people to consider a more realistic alternative lay at the heart of their work. The trainers would go along and ask what the difficulties were. Perhaps it was bad water and people needed a well. Perhaps it was poor education and they needed a school. Then they would ask what their resources were and invariably get the reply, "None".

That was where the enterprise really began. What followed was a thorough discussion of what communal talent they could draw on. Could they get someone to provide the wood for a school room, could they pool their resources and buy the books, could they not draw on each other's goodwill and effort to do something modest for themselves, rather than wait for something grand from someone else? To mobilize the corporate muscle and will involved changing the way decisions were generally made. In the past, village or tribal elders would decide what needed to be done and tell everyone to do it. The only way villagers could say No was simply to do nothing. And so nothing was done. When the laity training team arrived, the first task was to put these ancient and accepted patterns of leadership under scrutiny, so that ordinary people could then be encouraged to have a stake in their future. Though few of them knew it, these were precisely the same adjustments which their English counterparts had been induced to make in, say, John Wilson's Bedminster parish four thousand miles away, and, whether in the lush pastures around the Cheddar Gorge or in the tropical heat of East Africa, the principles involved remained identical. "What Terry and I were trying to do was to harness human resources as well as financial ones", says Philip Turner. "It was a case of getting things done by getting people to know that they could do them. And in this Terry had enormous natural ability."

When the Waites flew out, now with a third young member of the family, Gillian, they stayed first with the Rev. and Mrs Hutchison of Makerere University. Later they moved on and settled at Mukono, the theological college where Eric Hutchison, a Canadian, worked. His wife, Elspeth, remembers a fresh-faced and beardless young man, friendly and full of jokes. A dominant image of the time is of him striding into the room bearing shoulder high a twin on each arm. With twin girls of her own, Elspeth Hutchison remembers a full house of youngsters and busy times for everyone. "Frances must have had a busy time packing up at home, and I was aware of how exhausting the whole business of finding yourself suddenly transplanted to a foreign country actually is. Even then, though, it was quite clear that she coped splendidly with everything. She is a quiet person, perhaps a shy person and very reserved, and I think she always knew that Terry was the sort of person who had to be out and about doing things. It must have been extraordinarily hard for her at times, but she has deep reserves of hidden strength which I don't think many people have appreciated."

Terry himself kept in frequent contact with Eric Hutchison, but when the Waite family shortly afterwards moved twelve miles to the other side of Kampala, to Bishop Tucker Theological College, Elspeth saw the family less often. But powerful first impressions – later backed up by experience – have remained. "What struck you about Terry was this overwhelming sense of treating everybody as an individual in his own right. From the house boys, in whom he took a real interest, to the Archbishop, he dealt with everyone as a person on an equal footing. He took people seriously and this was appreciated."

Gordon Kitney, who followed his career in Uganda closely, bears it out. "With Terry keeping an eye on operations, the Church could develop a proper sense of missionary zeal. Now I don't mean that in an abrasive way, at all. It simply means that people could be trained to function more ably and to take the Church out to people in an active and effective way. You see, at the bottom of all this is a simple fact. The Church can either be welcoming or not, and that's a quality above and beyond abstract notions of mission. And Terry, wherever he travelled, opened it all up to everybody, welcoming them wherever he went. The people he met he recognized as being in God's image, and he responded to them, in faith, as individuals, whatever tribe, class, religion or colour they happened to be. And he dealt with the whole person, not part of it, never neglecting the physical needs they had at the expense of the spiritual."

The hilltop at Namirembe lived up to its name as "the place of peace". Disruption, shootings, political upheaval and civil war in the area provided a terrible backdrop to the latter part of Terry Waite's time in Uganda, but in the mission community around the Cathedral, at least, some sort of order could prevail. Gwen Oliver, a doctor's wife and close neighbour of the Waites, looks back as if to a second Eden. "Uganda is so green and the hill is so beautiful. For years they'd imported these glorious bougainvilleas. You could come across a hedge of seven or eight different colours, and then there was hibiscus in every shade from apricot to blue. We had guavas and paw-paws, pineapples and mangoes, and masses and masses of bananas growing in the gardens right in front of us. And a lovely little blue flower called 'yesterday, today, and tomorrow' grew in profusion all down the side of the hill." It was to be here that Terry Waite, Frances, and the three children eventually moved to a modern house half- way up the hill behind the provincial offices of the Cathedral, and on the occasions he was not travelling enormous distances to far out places, more often than not in a sturdy Peugeot estate car, Terry Waite could enjoy some of the community life and take part in the regular rituals.

"We had a car rota for the children", says Gwen Oliver. "It involved four journeys a day because we had to bring them back for dinner, and Terry used to pile his car up with as many as would go in and ferry the lot to school. The kids loved him because he didn't just drive them there; he entertained them as well, telling them shaggy dog stories and jokes that had them in fits of hysterics." Much is made of the Waite humour, with its propensity for silly jokes and good-hearted nonsense, but few can remember actual examples of the future envoy's wit and repartee. Or is it that they dare not? On the understanding that jokes do not travel at all well, and that what brought laughter into being at the time can rarely be reproduced on the cold, white page, I offer you now a sample from the Oliver household, the story which Gwen's son can still hear with affection twenty years on. "Question: A prisoner lies in a cell without doors or windows. How does he escape? Answer: He rubs his hands until they are sore, with the saw he cuts the table in two, he puts the pieces together and makes a

whole, he jumps through the hole and shouts until he is
hoarse, he leaps on the horse and rides away." My
apologies to Terry Waite if I have chosen a less than perfect
vintage, but in its favour the joke, at the time, had a
receptive audience – a car full of children who adored him
for it and squealed for more.

For the rest of the day there was much to do. When times
were peaceful walks round the hill, prayer meetings and
shared suppers at each other's homes, or trips into the
Ugandan countryside, filled the time. Terry Waite, despite his
long absences from home, is always regarded as a family
man. Some friends have felt resentful on Frances' behalf that
she has had to endure countless days apart from him looking
after the children alone in foreign parts. And then again
others have referred to the time they did spend together as
"quality time", important and nourishing for its intensity,
not for its duration. The children, so the reports go, have
always been overjoyed to have their father, so loving and
entertaining a man, back in the fold. More recently Terry
Waite himself has referred to them as "a pretty tough group"
who take the enforced absences marvellously. Of his children
he is pleased to say that nothing he does can possibly be made
to impress them. But it is from his secure family life, all are
agreed, that he himself draws comfort and strength for what
has of late become hazardous work.

Though the training groups were in essence those of the
Bristol years the circumstances were often far more demanding. Again they were unstructured, and again the
important thing was not so much the content as the process. It was a way of developing communication and
understanding how decisions get made at all. Earlier the
tendency had been for the African to defer to the
European, and for the European to set the agenda. The
roles were being reversed, with the missionary trainers

prepared to progress at the pace of the Ugandan church and learn from it. But the good trainer needed to be very watchful because sessions based on "group dynamics" could be very destructive unless they were properly led. If people were encouraged to say what they felt, much hurt could be generated and much damage done. Some people might find themselves pushed beyond endurance, and others might store up great reserves of anger, so Terry Waite and other trainers needed themselves to be trained to keep a watchful, tactful eye on every step of the proceedings. And working within these groups was revealing not only to the trainees but to the trainers themselves a darker side of human nature, a side to which Laurence Reading had seen Terry Waite more than once exposed.

Those who assume that a naïve man unaware of the grimmer side to humanity made his way innocently to the world's trouble-spots are forced to review their assessment of Terry Waite. Many have said that he is oblivious to the negative aspects of human personality, and sees only the good side of people who are far nastier than they seem. There may be some truth in his readiness to seek out what good there is in people but it would be wrong, says Laurence Reading, to assume that he has no inkling of how the fallen world behaves. "I remember we organized one training group and had people sitting around in concentric circles, with Terry sitting on the outside. Now, at moments like this all sorts of things are going in a group. Sometimes an individual is set up as the fall-guy, or someone else is made to look the clown, or someone else is the weak one. What's happening is that it's often very difficult for anyone to behave as a totally free individual because of all the group pressure on him. It's rather like the novel *Lord of the Flies*. That's how people behave in groups, and Terry knows that. And the bigger the group the greater the forces and the more difficult it is to handle them. I would think we had forty or fifty sitting in the circles when, for no apparent reason, old Terry stood up and began to walk round the outside, very slowly, without saying a word. You could almost feel the tension rising. What is this chap going to do? His powerful physical presence, coupled with his childlike nature, suddenly became impossible to disentangle and had a tremendous effect. And suddenly this man whom everybody knows and likes becomes a very threatening figure. Now Terry knew how easily hostility could be generated and he was perfectly aware that all men are *not* good."

If the process Terry and others were exporting to another country seemed a dubious one and one potentially destructive in nature, that was to see only part of its purpose. It could, according to Elspeth Hutchison, have great and beneficial effects when used in a Christian context. "When people did get angry they were then able to experience deep forgiveness from the group. In many ways the profound Christian concepts of penitence, atonement and Resurrection came alive before your eyes in gatherings like these. The results were creative, not destructive." It seemed fitting to the people who attended the courses that if the end result was a Christian advance of some kind – whether for theological education, or for mission buildings or whatever – then the procedures by which the aims were achieved should also be rooted in the faith. This whole period was important because decisions were being taken which would affect the way the whole Church moved forward. Although Terry Waite was an adviser to the first black Archbishop, The Most Rev. Erica Sabiti, the Church, by and large, tended to be fairly white-dominated and here was the opportunity for the complete handover to be made.

"It was an attempt to see people on the footing of equality much more," says Eric Hutchison, "an attempt to view things from the African perspective, to discuss things with a greater frankness. That traditional respect which the older African would give to the older European could often mask a lot of deep-seated differences, and these needed to be aired. Where Terry's help was invaluable was in always being able to encourage this openness without anyone ever feeling they were giving offence. A joke or a laugh would disarm things in a flash, and he was always the one, in the very gentlest of ways, to point out what real feelings and opinions were being expressed beneath all the superficial things. Maybe he would point out to a bishop or an archdeacon that if they paused for a moment they would realize they weren't listening to what their junior colleague was actually saying. He would jump in, always with a smile, in a direct way which others might wrap up more politely. It was that strength and openness we valued." It was all redolent of the numerous sessions he and Laurence Reading had organized in England, when each would look at the other and ask the only genuine question there was to ask, "What's *really* going on here?" They could see what appeared to be taking place, but was it the whole picture? Learning how to spot what was *really* going on was part of the intuitive equipment he was refining during the whole of this period, equipment that would qualify him for much of the work which, as yet unknown, lay before him.

Meanwhile the stories which were reaching his Church Army colleague, Gordon Kitney, in England confirmed the society's own faith in his abilities. The talent to use words wisely was much praised as, too, was Terry's refusal to charge into a place and change tribal and village cultures to conform automatically to the European Christian model. He found in some remote spots, for example, that clergy poorly paid, and six or seven months behind in their salary, had taken to charging for Confirmation classes. A gentle word rather than a horrified reaction altered the position. Polygamy, though slowly dying out, was still sometimes practised. Curiously the first wife was allowed to join the Mothers' Union while the rest were not. It was Terry Waite's refusal to raise his hands in horror, as some may have done, which contributed to the mutual understanding he developed among those whom he met. "Terry was sensitive to foreign cultures," says Captain Kitney, "and he realized that if you merely stood up and said categorically, 'God says you must only have one wife', you automatically raised the issue of who was going to look after the rest. So with an eye on the distant objective of monogamy he accepted that there was no possibility of abandoning the traditions overnight." Economic factors were gradually instrumental in discouraging the practice, and indeed it was largely the Africans themselves, without outside encouragement, who were generally abandoning it.

But the point remains: that Terry Waite was there ready to accept the way people were, not the way they ought to be. It meant, for example, going along to the Mothers' Union service, watching the women file in in their blue and gold outfits, assist where needed, perhaps even talk at the service, all the time realizing that for every woman present there could be four more wives elsewhere. It meant accepting the culture. In the Baganda tribe, for instance, Gordon Kitney remembers, the tradition was for the men to eat first and women and children to eat what was left. Whenever the tall, by this time bearded, guest arrived he would ensure that he did not eat too much and thereby deprive the family. Sensitivity and understanding dictated everything he did, so that he might say to UNESCO or other organizations that dried milk was acceptable to the Baganda tribe while eggpowder was not, because their belief is that eggs cause infertility in women. The unwary could fall into traps.

As did Lena Waite, though not catastrophically, when she paid a three-month visit to Kampala to see her son – an incident she now recollects with some amusement. "The Mothers' Union wasn't far from Terry's house. It was a lovely brick building, with a beautifully laid out modern kitchen. They asked me to be the speaker while I was there and to address them about this and that. I used to go along and show them a little cooking and so on. I went along one day and gave them my demonstration, and when it was over went back to the house. Terry asked me what I'd been up to and I told him I'd been showing the ladies there how to scramble eggs! You should have seen the look on Terry's face. Mind you, they ate them all right and looked as if they were enjoying them, too!"

Laurence Reading recalls how Terry adapted himself to the customs of the land, and how he took to them all with relish. One year he flew out to see his protegé on Ugandan soil and was to be met at Entebbe Airport by Terry and Philip Turner. There was much to talk about – how the courses were progressing, how political developments were affecting them, for example, and how each was faring – but before the conversations proper got underway Terry insisted they all do it the African way and sit themselves beneath a large tree. "That was the traditional way to do it, that was how Terry did it. He excelled at that sort of thing and it was all great fun. Making an occasion out of something. That was his style, enjoying life but not necessarily taking it lightly."

He took life easily, but never for granted, and Oliver Tomkins remarked of him, "He clearly understood that to be a good Christian layman didn't primarily mean being busy. Rather it meant having depth, and unless you had spiritual roots and made time for quiet all your activity would be futile." It is an observation that provides an interesting balance to the popular notion that Terry Waite, the trouble-shooting envoy with a mission, is never still.

It is a not uncommon experience for a journalist to report events which are barely recognizable to those who are at the very centre of the events described. It is a common enough phenomenon in Northern Ireland, for example, or, for that matter, in any part of the world where one has to live one's daily life against a background of tension and violence. Reporters report the dramatic events while those most affected by them register only the day-to-day ordinariness of carrying on with life. So it was on Namirembe Hill in the latter part of Terry Waite's time in Uganda. The trouble which was in the air was the prelude to the coup in 1971, which saw Idi Amin take power from Milton Obote and open yet another chapter of suffering in Uganda's troubled history. However, Gwen Oliver reacted with a mild sense of disbelief. "When the worst of it was reported on the BBC World Service it was always in Kampala that it seemed to be happening. And yet it was very paradoxical that we were living here not realizing. There was a degree of unreality about it." It was an unreality gradually dispelled when the stealing of cars at gunpoint no longer became much of a talking point. Terry Waite himself had two cars taken in this way – the second from outside his garage close by the cathedral. It was at about this time that his nightly patrols to check the houses of the single missionaries began to be appreciated.

The trouble that he and colleagues from the medical, ecclesiastical and academic worlds had been involved in hitherto had not been confined within the Ugandan borders but stretched beyond as well. A civil war in Sudan had been fought for over a decade, and the casualties from the south streamed over the frontiers into the country, creating a refugee problem whose humanitarian appeal did not go unheard by those with some measure of influence and goodwill.

An ad hoc group of such individuals, based initially at and around the university, was assembled by a philosophy professor by the name of Storrs McCall, a cousin of Eric Hutchison. It was established initially to provide medical assistance to the southern Sudanese, in an attempt to counteract the epidemics of measles, smallpox, sleeping sickness and cholera that were ravaging the population. The operation also involved a number of initiatives to help them grow their own food within their country. But whatever efforts were made to make life more bearable were being simultaneously undermined by the seemingly endless civil war between the north and the south. The war had its roots way back in history, in a complex and uneven development of political power, economic reform, and religious and cultural influence. The southern population, numbering some four million in the early sixties and feeling themselves much the downtrodden "partner" in an unfair distribution of resources and power, were scattered over 350,000 square miles of territory in which there were only some seven miles of tarmac. Impassable because of seasonal flooding, the terrain was ideal guerrilla country. It was the southerners who had taken a severe beating who crossed the borders into Uganda, but the war took its toll on both sides. If emergency aid was important, peace was vital.

The World Council of Churches became involved in efforts to mediate between the two sides, and sent a mission to the north to investigate. What alarmed those at the university was that the contact between mediators and fighters was not evenly distributed. Storrs McCall and others despaired of any lasting peace agreement if the WCC met only one party to the conflict. The essential thing was to get the church representatives to meet those from the south as well, and the person instrumental in finding the way to pull this off was Terry Waite. That, at least, is the recollection of Dr Louise Pirouet, a lecturer in religious studies at the time, and an active member of the Sudanese emergency aid programme. If the Archbishop of Uganda, Erica Sabiti, who was head of a member church of the Council, could be persuaded to invite them down they could barely refuse, and the prospect of both sides meeting on neutral ground with independent mediators could give peace a healthy chance. Many more people were involved in the eventual negotiations which led to a peace agreement in early 1972, but in Dr Pirouet's view Terry Waite's intervention was crucial. He had the confidence of the Archbishop and knew the mechanism by which the World Council of Churches could be persuaded to come to Uganda to meet all players in the drama, and as a result she had the opportunity to see Terry's strengths in action on a much wider stage than he himself had trodden before. "He was sensible and wise. One had a sense that he didn't act precipitately but that he could act fast. One felt he knew who to trust and who not to." She adds, parenthetically, without being asked about current events in the Lebanon, "I think he got caught out this time."

The whole essence of trust, however, involves a risk. One hundred per cent guarantees of certainty, safety, and success would render the virtue of trust redundant. Why bother embarking on the adventure of faith if you have a watertight contract on the future, signed and sealed, in the palm of your hand? "I remember him saying to me that unless one behaved openly and honestly there could be no way forward, and that sometimes one had to risk it to make any headway at all. I remember much later in England he often repeated it, that sooner or later you have to trust someone. If he's wrong, that's part of the risk, isn't it?"

That Terry Waite did not always play safe is illustrated by an incident which took place on the day of the coup. There had been shooting around Kampala, and a friend of Louise Pirouet whose husband was away in Nairobi was left alone in the house. "I think we were all worried about her because she was not what you would call a practical person, and we weren't quite sure how she would react in an emergency. It was quite easy for me to see her by slipping round the hedges on the hill where we lived. So I went to check up on her and, of course, Terry had to be there, didn't he? Having driven right across the city in his Peugeot car. He was quite cheerful and I suspect he half-enjoyed it."

In Dr Pirouet's view the circumstances of those uncertain days had a lasting impression on Terry Waite and lent to his character traits which, while apparently opposite, can be seen to spring quite reasonably from the particular conditions he was working under at the time. She sees no contradiction, for example, in the gregarious Terry Waite and the loner, Terry Waite the family man and the roving, independent man of action. "You're solitary only through force of circumstance. If you're involved in some sort of risky operation involving other people then you have to learn to keep your mouth shut. We all learnt that in Uganda. If you're in a hotel you learn to sit where there's so much music you can't be overheard. You look around to see if anyone's listening. You don't tell anybody anything, and what living in places like that has done is, to some extent, to make us all very solitary. But I think you can't really be solitary without having your roots somewhere else. I think Terry's are with his faith and his family, from whom he draws the support to move out."

But Louise Pirouet, like others before her, has never failed to acknowledge that convivial half which is the serious mediator's constant companion. He is known to like his food and his drink, to enter into the spirit of the social occasions with all the considerable joie de vivre he can summon. No meal with Terry Waite is eaten without other people in the restaurant turning round to see where the laughter is coming from, and the parties, from Bristol to Uganda, have been the showcases for his simple, unself-conscious enjoyment of life.

In Uganda, meanwhile, Terry Waite's employment was coming to an end. His work in the training of the church people had brought him into constant contact with Roman Catholics, some of whose missionary societies abroad recognized in him the ideal figure to reorganize their own work in the light of the new spirit of religious enterprise and renewal in the wake of the Second Vatican Council. As in Bristol, three years earlier, there was no visible monument to his achievements left behind. Any impact he could have hoped to make was incalculable, providing not so much a great influx of physical or financial resources as a stake in the country's development and a down-payment on the Church's future.

6

REDISCOVERY

There was one important item to pack into the already laden Volkswagen bound for Europe. It was a small wicker basket containing the latest arrival to the household – a young son, Mark, delivered by Terry Waite himself some months earlier, and far too young to appreciate what new experiences lay ahead for him and the whole family as it cut its permanent link with one continent and prepared to settle in another. From Kampala they drove to Mombasa and then, partly by way of a holiday and relaxation, sailed round Africa for a month before docking, in an uncomfortably cold winter, in Spain. A boat took them on to Trieste and a plane brought them finally down to Rome. Terry Waite had planned to stay for two years, but ended up staying there for almost seven.

Flat 17a, Via San Bernadette, was part of a five-storey apartment block situated in a cosmopolitan, residential area a short drive from the Vatican. It was owned by the Medical Mission Sisters, an international community of trained and qualified doctors, nurses, pharmacists or hospital administrators who had chosen the religious life. Their Superior General at the time, Sister Jane Gates, an American, met the family at the airport and conducted them to their new home. She herself has vivid memories of the initial shock with which the children viewed such novelties as the lift – quite unknown to them in Uganda. And when they rushed out through the kitchen door to find themselves three storeys up in the air, they barely believed their eyes. There was a further phenomenon which needed some preliminary adjusting to. On the first evening Sister Jane took them back for supper to the Sisters' House. Mark was transferred to a large laundry basket, and the three girls followed with varying degrees of expectation and inquisitiveness. There was something strange, but they could not decide what it was until one of them ventured the necessary question, "Daddy, why are there no men here? Why are there no other daddies like you here?" Sister Jane heard, with some amusement, an attempted explanation from the father, but she is sure they were unconvinced by it and still in the dark about the new kind of world into which they had now moved. Language problems were not an issue. The international congregation of nuns used English as the lingua franca, and they would see to all the necessary practicalities which the Italian landlord might raise.

Settling down into the new routine was quick. The sisters helped to fill the flat with furniture, and an early arrival to the apartment was a second-hand television set, which worked a near hypnotic effect on the three girls. "They never took their eyes off that set when Terry walked in with it", says Sister Jane. "He balanced it on the table, and the girls took their seats on the three solitary dining chairs and sat in a row glued to this wondrous machine. If they got up they moved backwards so as not to miss a moment." These were all part of the new way of life to which the whole family was now becoming accustomed. The girls were sent to St George's, an English school which transplanted the English educational system to the heart of the Italian capital. The staff there today remember the girls as "remaining very English", despite their European surroundings. As a parent Terry Waite himself was described as sympathetic and co-operative, but in the end, for once, stood out little in a small community comprising some sixty nationalities and attracting parents who were all, in their different ways, special. What did mark him out as something of a talking point was the London taxi which he bought in England and drove over to Rome. It was, he said, the only vehicle comfortable enough to allow him to squeeze into it his ample frame AND give him enough space to load in all the children. Pulling up at points throughout the city, and driving apparently on the wrong side, invariably drew stares and comments.

The flat provided the base for his international operations, and whenever he was back there Sister Jane remembers he always made an effort to do something special with the family. "He was a wonderful father. On the occasion he was back he would arrange lots of different outings to the park or to the sea shore, always treating the time as very precious. I always felt he conveyed to them this strong feeling that whatever they did was important, that their school grades or their swimming lessons or whatever else were something he really cared about." The time together as a family was indeed precious, as it was, necessarily, limited and defined by the rigorous international schedule the new work demanded. Even cross-country treks through Uganda clocking up thousands of miles could not compare with the requirements of the itinerary drawn up by the Medical Mission Sisters. With houses in the Philippines, Indonesia, Pakistan, Bangladesh, Ethiopia, Kenya, Uganda, Malawi, South Africa, Swaziland, Ghana, Latin America, Germany, England, Holland and the United States – all of which were to be visited – the new occupant of the post had to be prepared to go anywhere at short notice.

Sister Jane had first met Terry in Uganda, where the by now legendary "group dynamic" sessions were being put into action at one of their hospitals. Those unfamiliar with the new techniques were, to say the least, surprised at what was being required of them. "He had given us all rolled up newspapers and instructed us to whack each other on the back of the legs. I think the point was that he was trying to see what kind of anger or irritation he could elicit. So he would call out, 'You're not hitting hard enough! Really give them a good hard whack!' Meanwhile he sat back enjoying it all enormously, and quaking with laughter at our inability to hurt one another!"

The spectacle of a congregation of nuns, sleeves rolled up and armed with folded copies of the *Uganda Argus*, trying to bash each other round the calves, may not suggest missionary work of great seriousness, but that is to mistake the point of it. Following the Second Vatican Council there was an urgent need to reform the way in which the Roman Catholic societies and institutions functioned. "Formerly", says Sister Jane, "we had lived in an authoritarian system with superiors and subjects. If people needed something they couldn't or wouldn't do it themselves, they'd go ask Mother Superior. After our re-newal meeting in '67 we were supposed to negotiate amongst ourselves. Well, you need skills for that. If you're put in a very rigid structure and then the structure is removed, many people find it hard to cope. They have to learn how to assert themselves, if necessary, and learn how to negotiate by themselves rather than by the rule book." This is where the folded newspapers came in. Here was one flippant but effective method of breaking down barriers within the hierarchy. Jane Gates herself had employed him, and realized the surprise that might be caused by taking on an Anglican, and a married man with a family at that, to run the nuns' training. "We developed his job description together and he reported to me, but we didn't employ him for any other reason than that he had this vast experience in this sort of work. The fact that he was an Anglican didn't really come into it. It's true that some people couldn't understand the reasoning at the time, but they were always totally charmed by him and hugely impressed by his sheer expertise."

The enterprise was given the title "Project Rediscovery" by the sisters themselves, who realized that crucial commitments had been made by Vatican II and there was a need for personal and institutional renewal throughout the whole of the Roman Catholic Church. Terry Waite's role was to be an instrument whereby they could be brought into greater touch with themselves as Christian women, and co-operate in the shared responsibilities of general administration.

Jane Gates' successor as Superior General in 1973 was the Dutch sister, Godelieve Prové. She took over at a time when their international meeting, the General Chapter, was scheduled to take place. It was a time to evaluate all the achievements so far and to look forward to the next six years of work. "Terry had worked with us for three years," she says, "and we decided that one more year would consolidate his work, and then we would be on our feet and able to carry on alone." Professional and personal contact was very close during these years, and the images Sister Godelieve retains from the times she visited the family at the Via San Bernadette exemplify the personality and the qualities of their much loved employee. Each child would be taken seriously as an individual, each one would be assigned a specific task as a host when a newcomer arrived. Ruth might take the coats, Clare might offer the tea, Gillian serve the cake. "Everyone was part of the total," she says, "everyone was important. And in that moment I realized Terry's gifts. Here was a model of how he dealt with people all around the world – of whatever culture, of whatever religion. Whether people came to him with belief or disbelief I think he saw in them their tremendous, yes, I would say, infinite potential."

Describing his impact on the communities he visited is not easy. As a friend put it, "Anything that Terry does is hard to put into words. It's not like a production chart where you can measure success on a graph. It is a never ending process involving more and more development as a person, greater and greater commitment as a Christian." Sister Sheila Collins worked in Western Kenya in the early seventies at a small mission hospital, which over the past years had seen changes so great in the organization of the religious societies that morale was low. Before Vatican II there had been a much more monastic way of life with a highly structured community lifestyle. They would work, pray and eat together, with even the formal recreation time compulsory on all. The lines of communication worked from the top downwards, and as a mission they tended to be merely a group of expatriate sisters who kept themselves very much within the enclave of hospital and convent. They worked hard, often doing several jobs at once, and some of them felt, in retrospect, that their very professionalism as medics, which was the initial reason for their foundation over sixty years ago, was a barrier between them and the people they served. As the Mission Hospital grew, the running of it became more and more complex.

"Bits were being added on here and there," says Sister Sheila, "and the whole thing was growing like Topsy. But the organization of the hospital doesn't necessarily keep pace with that, and lines of communication which are very simple on paper end up extremely complex. When the hospital secretary is also the social worker, and the pharmacist is also the hospital secretary the whole organization breaks down. There really was chaos and confusion within the outwardly quite formal structure." What the Second Vatican Council provoked were changes in leadership. Instead of being told what to do sisters were expected to participate more in the running of their own houses. Adapting to the new system was not easy, and the requirements of the time were for people's talents to be drawn out of them and for their confidence to be lifted. It was with these aims in mind that Terry Waite's training sessions were devised.

The technique was by now familiar. Taking a role which did not intrude on the action, he was able to observe what was going on, what games people were playing, how the articulate were inadvertently (sometimes deliberately) dominating the reticent. Then once a session was over he could play back to them everything he had seen, and ask for their reactions. Far from being merely theoretical exercises they had great practical relevance to the work at hand. "In the early days of mission, the attitude of the European", says Sister Sheila, "was to take the dominant role in helping those poor people 'somewhere out there'. Now there is much more a sense of co-operation, of equal partnership in a shared venture. What Terry helped us to do was to give us the confidence to help local staff, from Kenya to the Philippines, to assume leadership, authority and responsibility in our hospitals."

The theory, for some, was heavy going, and the implications were threatening, but those who met him at the hospitals were captivated. His respect for the religious traditions he himself did not share was constantly in evidence. "Appreciative of the positive in people", is how one sister at the time described him. Much earlier in Bristol Basil Moss had spotted those very qualities. "He was

101

supremely happy with a team and anxious to get people to work in teams. He was always fighting the kind of 'pecking-order' management styles which, he said, brought nothing of the real person out. He recognized that reorganizing the way you've done something for decades can be a painful business, but it was all done with as much participation, consultation and sensitivity as possible."

For many of the sisters the reorganization of the accepted structure was a crossroads in their lives, for some the most serious challenge to their vocation they had ever encountered. To enter the convents and the mission hospitals when many women were re-evaluating their most cherished beliefs called for tact and sympathy of a high order. In Manila, Sister Victorina de la Paz recalls the sensitive encouragement he gave them all when he first arrived. "Although not a priest he told us how much he valued the life of the religious. 'Stay in', he said gently but firmly, and his words were of great encouragement to those of us who felt our vocation wavering. His benevolence and his talent for reaching the most traditional of us and the most modern were very attractive."

Another quality which won them over to him strikes perhaps a strange note in a man so used to moving in and out of all kinds of experiences in all kinds of places. They noted a strange vulnerability. "He always needed lots of reassurance, and many a time", said one sister, "he would come up to you after a group session and say, 'How did it go? Did it go well?'"

The short answer to that question seemed to be in the affirmative. One of the Society's District Superiors, Sister Kathleen Brown, singles out another easily overlooked reason for his success, bringing to her judgement a perspective which only she could dare acknowledge. "I admired his ability to stay in the background and keep his mouth shut. And that, among a group of women, is quite difficult, I can tell you. But all the time he was silent he was listening – able later on to pick out the essential thread that linked all our remarks. There was an element of surprise when we first knew an Anglican was to come and help us out. The fact that he was married made no difference, nor did the fact that he was a man – the Church has been male-dominated for two thousand years. We're used to that!"

Pleasing such an international society was not a simple job to take on. The sisters admitted they ALL had ideas of their own, different backgrounds and different outlooks on the world. A pioneering society such as the Medical Mission Sisters attracts by its very nature independent-minded people. When the Society was founded by Mother Anna Dengel in 1925 religious sisters were not allowed to practise medicine. She herself in her time had been an innovator, and one prepared to take a risk against heavy odds. Now over half a century later another innovator was stepping in, in the form of a married Anglican male. She was alive at the time of Terry Waite's appointment, and apparently happy with all he did. "That", said Sister Sheila, "was the final seal of approval."

Those who met him at the time, on foreign soil or on home ground, remember the mild sadness of his departures. Usually a party would be held in farewell and, as if they had not guessed it already, the convivial extrovert part of his personality would bubble uncontrollably to the surface and leave them buoyed up with genuine elation. At one such farewell Terry Waite performed his party-piece, which involved standing on his head to the sung accompaniment of some now forgotten rhyme. Sister Sheila cannot remember why he did it, and for her it doesn't seem to matter. "That was Terry all over – a delight to be with and an important figure in many ways in all our lives. He set the ball in motion and once it had got going we were then ready to take over. Another image would be that of the sower. He sowed the seeds and then together we, and our mission work, reaped the harvest. We were rediscovering our purpose, rediscovering our vocation. To help us to do that was Terry's great mission."

All the while his work was not going unnoticed by other societies in Rome, who saw in this man not only someone of great ability but also someone with great access to the mission fields abroad – a man of wide international experience whom the Superior General described às "the very model of a trans-cultural person", someone at home within any geographical boundary. In off-duty moments they are credentials which doubtless commended him for membership of the Travellers' Club when he returned to London. As a set of professional qualifications they are precisely the recommendations for the job he later took up in Rome, when the work with the Medical Mission Sisters came formally to an end.

The *Servizi Documentazione e Studi* organizaton, SEDOS, as it was known, had good use for a man like Terry Waite in the late seventies. Here was an umbrella organization serving a number of Roman Catholic missionary societies, providing them with information, research material, facts, figures and statistics to help them in their work. The aim was to avoid endless duplication of filing systems, contacts and missionary documentation scattered throughout the city, by providing a central resource open to all. On the face of it the job on offer was desk-bound and full of paperwork. In practice, the work meant the same sort of travel as he had done before and involved sending reports back on conditions in the field. The value of the information was inestimable.

Suppose, for example, details were known of soil erosion in an area, or of plant experimentation, missionaries going out there would be in a position to know what to expect and how to deal with conditions they met. They might know that a change in the local diet had had beneficial or harmful effects, and could plan their own work armed with the information. Mission workers who could call on such agricultural research before setting out might in some cases be better informed than the local people in the area. They could then make a start on developments in, say, the water supplies, and through a series of small technological improvements allow local villages to solve their own problems before they themselves were even aware of how acute they might be. All these considerations would have a direct impact on the long-term survival of a community, and all would be on the agenda of the Church. Canon Samuel Van Culin, who was then running the World Mission desk of the Episcopal Church of the USA, saw a lot of Terry Waite when he made his frequent visits to mission centres in the seventies, and he compares this rigorously documented approach to the work with the Benedictine model of the Middle Ages. The Benedictines were developing their wide knowledge of matters great and small, and combined their life of prayer with an active concern for the world beyond the cloister. SEDOS may have had data banks where the monasteries had libraries, but the principle remained the same.

More than once he played host to Terry Waite in New York, when he stopped over on a trip which might take him from the Caribbean to Latin America and then on to Canada. The added bonus of having a man out in the field travelling so widely was that sometimes other societies, through the offices of SEDOS, might call upon his services and ask him to look in at one of their own local houses while he was in the area. So skilled was Terry Waite at a brand of on the spot reporting which he had almost made his own, that he did consultancy work in this field for other agriculture and relief organizations based in the city and beyond.

A revealing letter sent from South Africa to his friend Laurence Reading in England suggests a degree of impatience, not to say irritability, on Terry Waite's behalf, that his work seems to be less valued in his own country than it is on the European continent. "I have very little contact with England these days and wish it were better," he wrote in April 1976, "but it was so hard to stimulate any interest in what I was doing in Rome and so I tended to keep away." All the evidence was that foreign mission agencies valued his work enormously, and in the same letter he talks with enthusiasm of the variety of different church organizations prepared to fund and support him. It all points to what others had elsewhere suspected all along: that here was an internationalist thoroughly at home in the wide world, and arguably ill at ease within the known confines of his own national boundaries.

Another typical letter lists his breathtakingly involved itinerary. "I have just returned from the States, and the programme for the coming year looks interesting", he writes. His Philippines project is doing nicely, and, "in September I am back in the Philippines and India, and late November I am in West Africa." He adds that the next day sees a departure for Sicily – but this time, certainly to general relief at home, the six-week stay is to be a family holiday. "We need a good break," he writes with understatement, "and it will be nice to get out of Rome in Holy Year!"

The flat seems to have acted as a magnet for many of

Terry Waite's friends and relations who came out during this time to see him. A picture emerges of an immensely busy home life, radiating an atmosphere of welcome and warmth occasionally punctuated by mild eccentricity. Elizabeth Ralph, for instance, remembers a visit she made to Rome some time ago. Crossing the river and admiring the view she failed to notice a large bearded motorcyclist approaching her on the other side of the road. The motorcyclist, however, whose identity by now is surely not in doubt, was more observant; as he saw her he waved and shouted and, with little regard for the traffic, veered over the road and screeched his machine to a halt before inviting her along for supper. She adds with resigned incredulity, "I didn't like to ask him how he was managing to cope without any Italian. I just knew he'd get by and make himself understood somehow." Indeed, by some of those who knew him at the time in Rome he was known as the "Terry will fix it" man. There were those who sometimes thought his confidence excessive, that perhaps he was going too far out on a limb this time when he set himself and others goals to achieve in his mission work. But no one denies that his confidence, whether justified or not, had a habit of inspiring confidence in others.

A couple of years before eventually leaving Rome Terry Waite considered a career back in Britain as a mission director based in London, but he withdrew his name from the list of applicants and decided to branch out as a freelance consultant and retain his base in Europe. What finally prompted the move was the question of education for the children. The twins were reaching the age when they needed continuity at home, and so it was decided to bring to a close seven years of life in probably the busiest and most complex religious centre in the world.

With the children's education provided for, Terry Waite returned to London in characteristic fashion – taking a calculated risk on the future, with no promise of a permanent job and trusting that everything, in the end, would turn out right.

7

HOME

There is a popular rumour that Terry Waite was not in fact selected to be the Archbishop's adviser on Anglican Communion Affairs at all. The story, as persistent as it is difficult to substantiate, holds that he himself made the first move, notionally created the post, selected himself for it and made off for St Albans where the Archbishop-designate, Dr Robert Runcie, was then Bishop. Once there, he persuaded him of the need for such an adviser, convinced him of his suitability and, without further ado, moved into the first floor of Lambeth Palace to join the Archbishop's staff in 1980. It is a measure of Terry Waite's capacity to engender incredulous respect that many of his friends still fondly concede the possibility, even when the evidence suggests it is unlikely.

Canon Samuel Van Culin, now Secretary General of the Anglican Consultative Council, a body itself advising on and informing of development in the Anglican Communion worldwide, recalls that Dr Runcie had had some conversation with his (van Culin's) predecessor, Bishop John Howe, prior to appointing his personal staff. Dr Runcie was anxious to emphasize his relationships with the worldwide Church more, and to give more visibility to the goings-on in the Anglican Communion at large. For him to carry out this complex and demanding task alongside his many other functions he needed a reliable and informed right-hand man to back it up. The post which was devised grew out of the common thinking of a number of senior clergy at the time, among them Bishop Howe, and Terry Waite's former employer in Bristol, Bishop Oliver Tomkins. "I felt that one of the gaps in the structure of the Archbishop's staffing," says Bishop Tomkins, "was that he didn't have anybody to devil for him in international links with the rest of the Anglican Communion. He really needed someone whose primary job was to go and make preparations for him when he visited other parts of the world, to accompany him on his travels, and to follow up any developments." Certainly there was a need for at least another pair of extra hands at Lambeth Palace to help the Archbishop in what is, to some extent, three separate jobs rolled into one. First, he is a Diocesan Bishop, though the Canterbury Diocese recognizes that their claim on his attention must necessarily be limited. Secondly, he is Primate of All England, with enough domestic issues to keep him more than adequately occupied. And thirdly he has to keep an international weather-eye as President of the Anglican Communion. Clearly under any administration, and particularly under that of the "new man", there was a full-time job for the right applicant with the right qualifications.

When Terry Waite returned home in late 1978 he held a temporary job on the Africa Desk of the British Council of Churches. Staff there remember him as kind, courteous and efficient, a man who treated everyone with the same consideration. One secretary who worked for him at the time remembers with some surprise that he treated her as if she were one of his "senior clergy", rather than as someone "there to take notes and send out letters". But his time at the BCC is rather shadowy. He spent too short a period there for much real impact to be made. One close friend says that the unofficial reason for his leaving was the lack of job satisfaction in what was essentially a desk job. The huge amounts of paper work, in gross disproportion to the practical work, it was said, exasperated him, leading him later the following year to knock on Bishop Tomkins' door for his advice on how best his talents might be used.

It was late November in 1979 when he called on the Bishop, who was sympathetic, realizing that the obvious choice was for some kind of international job which would harness his accumulated experience to the full. "It takes years and years", the Bishop now says, "for such a store of experience to be assembled, and it would have been a great pity to have wasted it. I promised him I would keep an eye out for something. John Howe and I by this time reckoned that the way things were shaping up for the new Archbishop pointed to a gap in the staffing, which Terry seemed purpose-built to fill." John Howe, too, had been someone whom he had sought out for advice, so with these two powerful sponsors giving him their personal support the prospects for a permanent career looked favourable. Not that his appointment was anything of a foregone conclusion. Indeed Terry Waite, who knew nothing of the possible job at the time, was the embodiment of the casual approach to the enervating art of job application. It was a quality which impressed Bishop Howe. "What I found striking was the way in which he left Rome with no idea what sort of a job he'd do. He just trusted that something would turn up, and I for one was amazed that, in the end, something actually did. It was that sort of thing which surprised me. Things that would have daunted most people didn't bother him at all. He reckoned all would be well in the end."

Neither of his two champions had any intimation of the greatness in him. All recognized that solid expertise and global experience coupled with personal warmth and flair gave him outstandingly rare qualifications – but for what, no one was quite sure. Much earlier Basil Moss had put his finger on it. "I didn't know where he was going to go but I knew he was going somewhere. I didn't see in him greatness in any conventional sense." And at the time what also struck Bishop Tomkins was his readiness to serve. "I would describe him as totally unambitious as far as his own career was concerned", he says. "He was an adventurous man always looking for new fields to explore, but always harnessing that love of adventure to a real sense of vocation."

In April 1980, on a mild spring day in Rome, three men took a leisurely break for lunch. They had been attending a conference on Uganda at the Vatican, where Terry Waite had been asked along by John Howe for the benefit of his specialist knowledge. Samuel Van Culin completed the party, and the three set off from St Peter's Square, over the bridge by the Castel Sant 'Angelo, and sauntered down the Corso Vittorio Emanuele II in search of food. They settled on a small restaurant overlooking a garden piazza by the Chiesa Nuova, and sat down on the terrace beneath a coloured awning for an al fresco lunch. There was pasta and wine, but what impressed itself on Samuel Van Culin long after the menu had faded from his recollection, is the conversation he heard.

For the first time what had been a publicly unstated abstraction became an explicit possibility. If the post of Archbishop's adviser were to be created, asked John Howe, would Terry himself be interested? Samuel Van Culin noted the reaction. "He was very, very enthusiastic. John was acting as the intermediary here, sounding him out, as it were, and the response was favourable indeed." John Howe's role was by now almost over. He passed on the information to Dr Runcie, who at the time, he says, was noncommittal. "He wanted to see the chap personally and check him out before deciding if he would fit into the staff." Dr Runcie also sought the opinion of those who had known Terry both personally and professionally, among them Bishop Tomkins from the Bristol days. The memory of work done well clearly lingered, as a small extract from his testimonial of the time reveals. "He has gifts of personal charm which seem to guide him through many ticklish situations, combined with a soundness of judgement which is unusual in a comparatively young man. He knows how to work gently and slowly but with a firm sense of overall direction. He is physically tough enough to travel continuously, and with a wife and family who have come to terms with it completely, I think. This was well tested in Uganda, and the confidence of the Roman Catholic authorities in his work must be considerable for they have no wish to lose him. He is a convinced Anglican, all the surer for his close appreciation of and admiration for the Roman Catholic Church. He already has good ecumenical links in Geneva and elsewhere . . . (and) . . . we should be wasting a very gifted son of the Church if we can't find a billet which fully stretches him as an interpreter of Anglicanism." The job became his.

It was a very different job at first, however, from the one it has subsequently become. There was much liaison work between Lambeth Palace and the headquarters of the Anglican Consultative Council in Westminster. And as such it was a job hardly guaranteed to bring out the full battalion of the British and foreign press corps, but it was one which was greatly valued by Dr Runcie. By now his "noncommittal" reaction had turned, according to John Howe, to a great admiration for Terry's energy and ability, coupled with wry amusement at his habit of popping in at every office to see how work was progressing and checking that everything was running smoothly. There were faint echoes here of the confident lay trainer dashing with ease and eagerness from one group session to another but, as he did with the Medical Mission Sisters, always asking at the end of a session, with a surprising note of diffidence "How did it go? Did it go well?"

The post, which fitted him well enough to start with, he seemed gradually to be tailoring to his own requirements – a process with which his close friend and colleague Laurence Reading can easily sympathize. "He's almost always been something of a freelance with no real job specification as such. In that sense he's been very like me, and I feel very strongly with Terry over this because I've been fortunate with my jobs. But you can also get some hostility – I did from my fellow clergy. They didn't know exactly what my job was and they didn't like it either. People far prefer your job to be written down plainly in black and white."

And yet despite a certain distance he put between himself and others, he always belonged. He belonged, for example to the Anglican Church with whose "passionate coolness" he had instinctively felt at ease. The implicit contradiction is quite compatible with his own paradoxical personality, and suggests the need to be simultaneously part of and yet independent of any structure. His brother, David, understands it when, referring to the influence their father had on the household, he praises the freedom which can be achieved within known boundaries. Terry Waite himself recognizes it when he talks with some eloquence about the nature of Orthodoxy which he finds so appealing. The traditional, changeless liturgy could be thought by some to restrict the spirit. For Terry Waite (and for many, many more) it is a way of releasing it. It is as if by constant familiarity with the form the form itself vanishes, leaving only the process; the channelling of the spirit directly to

God. Terry Waite has often spoken of the beauty of icons in Orthodox worship. For him the icon of the Virgin Mary, for example, is representation and reality at the same time. It speaks, he has said, of a depth of love only women can know because of what they have to suffer for love. They have children needing constant attention, which forces their own feelings into the background for fifteen or sixteen years. Women, he says, are forever giving; giving to demanding children and demanding husbands so that they know so much more about sacrificial love than men ever will. So the icon represents the love of one special woman who gave birth to Our Lord, but is the embodiment of women's love in general.

The constant tension of opposites is a phenomenon Terry Waite seems always to have lived with: the family man who is rarely home, the man of action and the man of reflection, the team player and the solitary cyclist, the convivial host and the quiet loner. It was while he was in Uganda that he first began to read Jung and that, for many of his friends, began to make some sense of these contradictions. It is impossible to summarize the Jungian approach in a few words here (not least because of the limitations of this book's author), nor is it easy to apply the particular brand of psychological insight to an understanding of what makes the Archbishop's envoy the man he is. But let Samuel Van Culin, as a friend, not as a scholar, elaborate at some length here on the appeal he thinks Jungian study has for him.

"I think for a thoughtful sensitive man in his mid- to upper-thirties, living in a variety of different cultures confronted with a variety of religious qualities and questions of an emotional and psychological nature, the psychology of Jung affected him in a way other psychologists didn't. For one thing Jung takes religious experience seriously. He doesn't try to describe it as an after-effect of some other instinct or emotion. He is serious about religious mythology and the way in which religious problems can be a source of disturbance to them. I also think Jung's understanding of the archetypes helped to focus Terry's mind on underlying realities at the heart of or beneath religious symbols, customs and traditions. By archetypes I mean the patterns of response that lie at the very core of the human psyche. They are basic patterns that come out in symbols and tales, but if you dig down beneath them you will discover that there is a pattern underneath. One pattern, I'd say, might be the search for unity, an integration of opposites, those ideas, values and customs which on the *surface* seem to be in conflict. Dig down deeper and you will find the archetypal level from which they emerge, where they would be seen as integrated. The opposites might be Roman Catholic and Anglican; Western, Eastern; developed, underdeveloped; the collective world of the African tribe as distinguished from the individual world of the western man. I think discovering Jung was very important for Terry, in that it helped give meaning to things that until then appeared to be in conflict. For him it was a way of finding in that conflict the creative, a way of unravelling the puzzle. Terry takes God very seriously."

Could this perhaps explain his love of Orthodoxy, when he says that we want to see life parcelled up in neat packages (largely for security's sake) rather than as the mystery it is? Could it be that in the icons, the liturgy and the singing he perceives the very expression of the accessible and the impenetrable mystery of God – the puzzle and its resolution?

Alongside that inner life, of course, was the outer half of Terry Waite, never more approachable and at ease, it seemed, than when he was travelling round on behalf of the Archbishop preparing for visits here and engagements there. On one occasion, for example, just a few years ago, when he was accompanying the Archbishop of Canterbury to Africa for the enthronement of the present Archbishop of Uganda, he happened to bump into one of his former colleagues from Bristol, the Rev. (now Canon) John Wilson, who remembers well the circumstances of the meeting.

"The great thing about it was that we just carried on where we left off twenty years ago. It was so gratifying because although we hadn't seen each other for all that time, not even been in touch, it was as if we'd been in each other's company just days before. I mean, I'd watched him from afar with great interest but we had never made contact. Of course it didn't matter a bit. I remember he was wearing a white cassock and frequently going up to the Archbishop to have a word – while we waited in a queue outdoors for the food to be served. This attracted the attention of several Ugandans, who made a point of telling me that here was the Archbishop's bodyguard. They said, 'You see that very large man over there? The reason he's so huge is that he's covered in guns beneath that white cassock of his.' Later on as this great feast wore on I told him that lots of people here thought he was swathed in arms and armour and, of course, he bellowed with laughter and told me that it happened quite often. The point is that we were able to relax in each other's company immediately and there was no sense of standing on ceremony."

On another occasion Elizabeth Ralph remembers him returning fresh from China in readiness for the Archbishop's trip there, and all set on the very morning of his return to organize more arrangements. "There he was among all these high-powered clergy carrying out his job to perfection. And I remember saying to Bishop Oliver that he really does seem to be a man God is using. And he himself believed that God was directing him, that things were BOUND to be all right. And I also remember thinking to myself how wonderful it was that a man like Terry, who had had a limited formal education, could be doing what he was. I mean, it just goes to show that the intellectuals are not always the right people to do the job." It is an observation Dr Louise Pirouet, herself an academic, would support unreservedly. "If you're working under the conditions we were in Uganda, academic qualifications don't come into it. He could have had five degrees or none. I simply didn't ask because it made no difference at all to his qualities."

One small tale to conclude this transitional stage of Terry Waite's life. Transitional because so far his work as Dr Runcie's adviser had brought some celebrity, enough to enliven his life but not yet sufficient to influence it. As the nature of the job in hand changed so, too, did his attitude to it, and not, according to some of his friends, always for the better. But then there would be many who would argue that even this change in attitude was attributable in a large measure to his virtues rather than his failings. Obliging to press and cameras alike, always willing to help media men and women meet their deadlines and fill their columns, he was perhaps too ready to be at their calling and unaware how easily the medium could distort the message. But, for the moment, to the transitionary tale.

When John Wilson said he had not seen Terry Waite for twenty years he was omitting one brief moment. He cannot remember when exactly, but it was five or six years ago, when he had obviously been to a Royal Garden Party. It could well have been, though there is no one to corroborate this brief encounter, in 1982, when he received his MBE after success in Iran.

"I was driving by Buckingham Palace one afternoon and I saw him in his morning suit, or what have you", John Wilson says. "You couldn't mistake Terry, and sure enough it was him. And I thought to myself, 'Good, I'm glad you've been.' Because I think he would enjoy the occasion in the very best sense." And as he saw him there momentarily he was reminded of another moment fifteen years or so earlier, when he was the first to leap into Butlin's pool at Minehead and open the way for the rest to join him. "The smile on his face brought it all back", says John Wilson. "He must have had his sadnesses and his disappointments but that was something one never saw. He would always cheer you up. He was always smiling and, when I say smiling, I don't mean in a lighthearted way. I mean he'd radiate, well, goodness, really. He didn't see me as I drove past but I thought to myself, 'Good for you, Terry. I'm glad for you.'"

8

OUT

IRAN

In December 1980 Terry Waite became a world figure. Virtually overnight his status as a private, largely anonymous church diplomat was transformed. From now on he became public property, catapulted through force of circumstance into the centre of momentous events. On board the plane to Iran was the same Terry Waite who had run the Bristol laity training group, the same Terry Waite who had helped Ugandan priests and Roman Catholic nuns to develop their missionary work, but the circumstances in which he was playing this new role were of a different order. To this very point in history future generations would be able to trace the emergence of one of the most powerful and influential nation states in the Middle East in the twentieth century. For a man to make his mark on the world he needs to be in the right place at the right time. Terry Waite was there when history was being made. Even though in the context of the world drama this was no more than a walk-on part, for many in the audience he stole the show and seized their imagination. When the rest of the performance became too complex to follow, and when half the action was happening off stage anyway, his appearance by the footlights in a cameo role of the Anglican Church's own making humanized the show. When Terry Waite was out front, the audience sat up. And his stature as a performer grew by association with the principals.

The events inevitably coloured the man and sparked a succession of highly publicized mercy missions which will doubtless make history themselves, so it is worthwhile looking at the Iranian episode in some detail.

The Anglican Bishop of Iran, the Rt Rev. Dehqani-Tafti, and his family had sat out the first eight months of the Revolution with varying degrees of apprehension. Within a week of the change of power in February 1979 his senior priest was murdered in Shiraz, an event which as he now says "rang the first alarm bell". Within a month a group of Islamic "fanatics" who, he says, had been a constant source of trouble for the past twenty years, moved in to claim the fruits of newly acquired power. They expropriated two hospitals in Shiraz and other church land. At the time there was, according to the Bishop, some semblance of the law and order they had formerly known, so they consulted their lawyers and even appealed to Ayatollah Khomeini. They received little satisfaction. The intimidation from the gang gradually increased. They raided the house and the offices, and took away everything, from books to photograph albums, before setting light to some of the church files. Refusing to sign away the Church's property by signing a document which would have released the diocese's trust fund, the Bishop was taken to the Revolutionary Court in Isfahan where he feared the worst.

The worst nearly occurred in November 1979, when a group burst into his bedroom at dawn. His wife woke up first and saw the gunmen. They woke the Bishop (Islam forbids that you kill a man while he is sleeping), and pointed a gun at his head. His wife threw herself over him and five shots were fired. There was blood on the pillow. His wife screamed and ran after the men as they left, and when she returned discovered her husband alive. Four bullets had gone round his head and the blood was from her hand which had been the target of the fifth. They left the country to attend a conference in Cyprus, leaving behind confusion and chaos, which was to engulf the three British missionaries whose rescue Terry Waite was later to secure.

"Gosh, won't you find Iran dull after Israel?" said one of Jean Waddell's friends, as she prepared to leave Jerusalem in 1976 where she had been secretary to the Anglican Archbishop there. Her new post as secretary to Dehqani-Tafti of Iran was to involve her in excitement she could have done without. The first signs of that were apparent shortly before the Revolution.

"We had a sixty-strong choir at St Luke's made up of all different nationalities," she says, "and put on *The Messiah* just before Christmas. And then just a few weeks later we were invited to put it on again because it had been such a success. But there were only three or four people left. All the others, particularly the Americans, were withdrawn quickly when they saw trouble." The trouble had taken the form of mass anti-American demonstrations, with hundreds of thousands taking part. One particular incident which stayed with Jean Waddell was a demonstration involving students, middle-aged men, mullahs and other clerics riding motorcycles down the main street – a bizarre sight which lent an air of unreality to it all. By this time Bishop Dehqani-Tafti had left Cyprus and was in England, where he was advised not to return to Iran. Jean Waddell, who had been out of the country in Cyprus accompanying the Bishop at his conference, did return and realized that the very fabric of society was beginning to be transformed. A curfew had kept her overnight in Tehran before she was able to return to her home in Isfahan. Black holes which had been cinemas, burnt-out shells which had been supermarkets, greeted her on her return and spelled the end of anything "decadent" and western in the newly established Islamic state. It was when she began to help move the offices from Isfahan to Tehran that she herself became personally caught up in the trouble. As she opened the door of her flat on 1st May 1980 two gunmen entered and questioned her. Why was she, a foreigner, still around? Who was she? Where did she work? Not satisfied with her replies they knocked her out, tied her up, bundled her under an eiderdown and shot her. The "fanatics" then disappeared and police and ambulance arrived.

The first thing she remembers when she came to was the sight of burly Iranian policemen breaking down the door and calling for an ambulance to take her to the hospital, where she underwent emergency surgery. She was comforted by the Bishop's wife, who was shortly to receive more tragic news – that her own son, Bahram, had been shot dead. It was time for everyone to leave the country. In August, after Jean Waddell had recovered, she set out to get her exit visa in Tehran; but she was told instead to head for Isfahan where she was to be questioned. That was the beginning of her seven-month detention on charges of spying.

In Isfahan she was led to believe that the Church had been wiped out and that all her colleagues and friends, including Dr and Mrs John Coleman, the two other hostages, had been executed. "It was a living nightmare", she says, in words which echo, as Terry Waite knows full well, the plight of every hostage unjustly detained. "I had been in solitary confinement in the women's section of Evin prison and I had lost contact with the outside world." In December she managed to see an English edition of the *Tehran Times* and read that the Archbishop of Canterbury was about to send an envoy to help. In the intervening months since Terry Waite had been called from his holiday caravan in Norfolk, cutting short his stay to return to Lambeth Palace at speed, preparations for release had been laid. So it was that Terry Waite – in his new role of "special envoy", by which title he was generally to become known – set out on Christmas Eve on his mission to comfort and release the prisoners.

His first meeting with Jean Waddell is indelibly marked on her memory. "I was taken down to an interrogation centre, escorted by a guard who didn't seem to know herself where we were going. We went up and down stairs and I had no idea what to expect. Then this door opened and there was Terry. He's such a big man, with such a warm comforting presence, and he just clasped me to his bosom."

Here, perhaps, is the primary strength of the man. His mere presence. True, any mediator would have inspired relief and gratitude in a prisoner detained and isolated in a foreign country, but to say that does not detract from Terry Waite's qualities. It is his determination to travel out, at great personal risk, simply to *be* there alongside people, which gives hope beyond words to the hostages themselves. He knows that no letters of concern, telegrams of sympathy or reports of help can do what his presence can. In that sense he is not playing the role of mediator. He has become the means and the substance itself of mediation. To borrow an image from his beloved Orthodoxy: at the moment of encounter with Jean Waddell he had become an icon of Christian mediation – at once its representation and an instrument of its reality.

When that moment had passed the real world impinged again. As it always does. As Terry Waite knows it must. And the time for other qualities was at hand. "When Terry walked in," says Jean Waddell, "you could feel the suspicion of the Revolutionary Guards in the air. They had some hard things to say to Terry about their hostility to Britain and to the Church, but he simply listened. He didn't get belligerent or argumentative, he simply sat there, very intently, saying he would look into matters to see if there could be any substance to the charge. The two of them – Terry and the Guard – ended up speaking as friends." In practice Terry Waite was able to show that documents purporting to be from the Bishop's office were obvious forgeries, and thereby he managed to establish a defence, but it was personal quality as much as practical advocacy which had its effects.

On 14th February Jean Waddell was told that she was free. It was not the end of the ordeal. Expecting to meet Terry Waite, she was instead taken to a car park, put into a car with blackened windows, and taken to a detention centre in the woods for three days. Then she was blindfolded, driven into Tehran at midnight, and led into a room. When she removed the blindfold she was seated in a French antique chair, beneath a crystal chandelier, gazing at damask-hung walls. All the prisoners were there, safe under one roof. On 28th February they were back in Heathrow, accompanied by the Archbishop of Canterbury's Special Envoy, who modestly tried to hug the sidelines but who was inescapably pulled centre stage.

So how did he succeed? "The two-metre man", as he was known by the guards, had immense charm and was admired and liked by them. All this Jean Waddell can testify to. But she never saw him talking to those in high authority, with whom other qualities were clearly needed. Sincerity, humility, patience played their part as, too, did his non-political religious status, symbolized by his cassock, which he constantly wore. But was there more? His practical help in proving that the charges of spying were implausible must have established his reputation as a thoughtful operator on foreign soil, but it was essentially his position as a powerless man in the middle which gave him his standing. As a representative of a religious leader himself he could dissociate himself from the decadent western materialism with which a secular arbitrator might have been tarnished, and call on a vocabulary of faith similar to that of the Mullahs and the Ayatollah, in order to communicate with the country's leaders.

As those who have followed Terry Waite's career know, he is no stranger to Islam. He understands the nature of its society, its desire to see the law enshrined in everyday life. Both in Uganda and in his travels through Asia he has seen it at work and, being familiar with it, is not disoriented by it. He understands the religious in everyday life, and his understanding established his bona fides as a man of the spirit who, however remotely, had something in common with the leaders in Iran at the time. His unswerving belief in and care for the value of each of the missionaries' lives, when pressed home with firmness, humility, and transparent integrity, was guaranteed to appeal to the best in even the most intransigent of religious zealots. Of course, the appeal may have been guaranteed but success was not. That depended on many other factors. Not least, in this case, on the fact that the hostages were clearly innocent and caught up, in the first chaotic months, in tumultuous events which were often beyond the control of the authorities themselves. Those in positions of power in central government must surely have been open to the possibility that mistakes could have occurred. What is more, what possible propaganda or bargaining power could the detention of seven Anglicans (three British, four Iranian) have had in the framework of such radical domestic events? Here was a unique situation. It needed a unique figure –

with tact and firmness, humility and authority and, above all, total honesty – to succeed.

In between his missions, though, when he is not "out" as a special envoy, he is home as an ordinary family man, and his very ordinariness comes as a refreshing antidote to his concentrated commitment abroad. His cousin, John Waite, for instance, has memories of Terry's help as a handyman, although, from his description of the event, it is clear he brings to every job he does the same degree of high octane energy. John had just happened to move into a new flat when Terry had taken possession of his Blackheath home in South London. Both properties needed much work, but Terry decided to leave his own and help John with his – in particular with the tiling in the kitchen. It is John who picks up the story. "I had expected to take a while and do it 'artistically', but Terry wanted to do it all in a day. He arrived in the morning on his scooter, to find me cutting the tiles rather slowly. So then he joined in and accelerated the pace. I scored the tiles and he, with his massive hands, would whack them with a kind of karate blow and do the job in half the time. We didn't break for meals, just kept on with it until it was done. He arrived in a sort of whirlwind in the morning and left me in a daze of dust and debris in the evening. But we finished the job."

A similar thing can be expected when he pays visits to his relatives. He hates to stay cooped up (a thing his friends feared most for him in his own incarceration in Lebanon); instead he wants to be out walking in the park, calling on friends, being active. His restlessness is legendary and compulsive. On one occasion, calling on his mother in Cheshire, he suggested they go out for a stroll. She accepted and put on some old shoes. Half-way into the walk he had a change of plan. Why not go to Southport? "Southport?" she said. "Well, I'll have to go back and change my shoes." But Terry wouldn't have it. There was no time to lose and they must be off. It was only after some persuasion that she succeeded in winning a few minutes' reprieve. She was allowed to change her shoes, and was taken off. Arrival and departure have become the twin watchwords of his life, and whether to Tripoli or to Southport the urge is always to move on.

There are, however, moments when even he has to stop, but rarely out of choice. As John Waite has seen, his hard work and concentration have sometimes exacted their price. "When things are moving to a critical point, you notice how physically tired he is. The last time he came round to my house was just before Christmas, shortly before he set off for Beirut this last time. He was sitting in the chair next to my mother, and when she got up to go I saw her out. By the time I had returned, within the space of a couple of minutes, he was asleep. And he stayed asleep for six hours in the middle of a Saturday." That, for a man who according to his brother, David, needs only four hours' sleep a night to get by, is surely evidence of concentration and application.

By common consent he is a man who prepares thoroughly for his missions, briefing himself exhaustively on the domestic situation of the country in hand but being, as he has constantly claimed, totally above the political arguments. For him the humanitarian is paramount and neutrality is his home ground. After the success in Iran, however, neutrality was more difficult to be *seen* to maintain. Not impossible, but infinitely more difficult.

LIBYA

The name of Terry Waite was known to Carol Russell, but she had not even considered that he might be able to help. It was her mother who made the first move. Carol's husband, Alan, an English teacher and occasional organist at the Anglican church in Tripoli, had been detained during a period of political upheaval in the Libyan capital in the late spring of 1984. There had been an attack on the army barracks, and security was more than usually intense. So, too, was the tension on the streets and, according to correspondents experienced in these matters, those who are foreign and vulnerable are very likely to run into trouble at such sensitive times. Alan Russell, Malcolm Anderson (an oil engineer), Michael Berdinner (a lecturer) and Robin Plummer (a telephone engineer) happened to be in just such a position and, hitherto unknown to each other, found themselves sharing a joint predicament. They had been arrested and were to spend the next nine months in detention.

Carol Russell's mother picked up the telephone and called Terry Waite. The appeal was direct. Can you help? He said he would come down to their home near Ipswich and talk it over. Carol Russell remembers the concern he showed, but in a way which was clearly not uncritical. "He spent a long time asking me questions about Alan to make perfectly sure that he could not have been arrested for any political reasons. When he was satisfied he agreed to help. It was a conversational meeting really. He had lunch with me and the children. I wouldn't say it was like an inquisition or anything, but he did want to know that there could be no politics involved." She was very impressed, and put her total trust in him. "I knew once I met him that here was a man who could accomplish something."

It is trust of that kind so completely surrendered that has continued to exert the relentlessly benign pressure on Terry Waite, and forced him to go on. By his own admission he sets out only when asked.

Carol Russell subsequently made contact with the families of the other detainees. From then on their futures were intertwined and their fears jointly shared. "Terry was straight with us from the start," she says, "and he told us that he would tell us what he could, that he might withhold certain things, but that whatever he did tell us would not be a lie. And we all appreciated that." Once he had accepted the request to help he had made his personal commitment to them and there was no going back. Those who advised him not to return to the Lebanon last time had to take that intimate personal involvement with the lives of the hostages there into account.

In both Britain and Libya the political temperature was rising. In England students had been arrested on terrorist charges and were later jailed. With the shooting of WPC Fletcher in St James' Square in 1984, relationships between the two countries deteriorated to such a point that diplomatic relations were severed, and the members of the Libyan People's Bureau expelled. In this political climate Terry Waite set off for Tripoli, fully aware of the strains which were inevitably going to be put on his humanitarian mission.

Those who watched him being shuttled between various Libyan People's Congresses as part of a well orchestrated domestic propaganda campaign despaired this time of his ability to find any common ground between himself and Colonel Gaddafi at all. But that was to reckon without the quality Laurence Reading had spotted much earlier. "It was that innocence coming out again, that determination to find something in this man that would bring about some sort of rapport or communication." Once more the appeal was to be to the one God of Christianity and Islam, and to the common humanity believers could share. He took with him a present for the Colonel, a scholarly work on the influence of Greek culture on Arab life in the seventh century, and spent a large part of the two-hour meeting on the afternoon of Christmas Day 1984 talking about the continuing relationships there should be between Islam and Christianity. Terry Waite has said that the Libyans spent a large part of the preliminaries sounding him out as to his real motives for coming to Libya, and deciding whether it was as a churchman or as a government representative. One of his persuasive speeches at the time, to a Libyan People's Congress, asserted his religious credentials and encouraged his audience to accept that, "Politics are made by men, justice and mercy by God."

It was an impressive attempt to find the common ground between himself and a man who considered himself, according to one correspondent there at the time, very much a philosopher king in his own land. Others, however, saw more pragmatic reasons behind Terry Waite's apparently successful personal persuasion. "Gaddafi was very conscious that he needed economic and educational ties with this country," said one source, "and that he desperately needed to get back on the right footing with Britain. He knew he would have no chance of that until the four were released, so he made sure they were released. But only after the endless and tedious window dressing of the People's Congresses."

Whether the Waite influence was crucial or tangential will probably never be known with any certainty. What is clear is that it was instrumental, in very important respects, in creating a climate of trust which was necessary before the detainees could be released. So delicate was that trust that the slightest provocation could upset it all. The decision to hold the memorial service for the murdered policewoman, when mediation seemed to be bearing fruit, was seen in Libya, according to Terry Waite, as just such a provocative act and threatened the success of the whole mission. He himself has said that at that point it was within an ace of failure, but that Colonel Gaddafi ultimately made the release on the grounds of personal trust and out of respect for the Archbishop of Canterbury's humanitarian initiative.

Basil Moss, as someone who saw Terry Waite's personality in action at close quarters when he was in Bristol says, "Talking to Gaddafi was entirely characteristic. On the basis that he belived in God, Terry would have thought it entirely appropriate to give him the credit for some sort of integrity and morality." Here was the example of the man looking for that spark of fellow-feeling in everyone and fanning it until it began to give off a perceptible heat.

The process was, of course, open to criticism, and at the time people said he had gone too far in appeasing a man whose actions could not be justified. He was criticized for involving himself (and the Church) in such craven self-abasement. But from the outset he had set aside any feelings for himself, and committed his efforts to serving others. He had made a personal pledge to them, and to refuse to mediate as he had promised, because he did not necessarily see eye to eye with the Libyans, would have resulted in prolonged detention and perhaps worse. It was a risk he could not afford to take. While he has shown courage in facing risks for his own sake he has never been happy to put other people's safety in jeopardy. Continuing the dialogue – at whatever cost in public contempt – was the only course open to him, the natural consequence of his having identified himself so intimately with the hostages themselves. One of his great strengths as a mediator, said one correspondent, is his perseverance. "He does keep channels open, and certainly in Libya, when all formal contact between Britain and the hostages was severed, this is important." If you are not a hostage you can afford to take the view (and it may be right) that talking to some regimes or individuals can only serve to give them a legitimacy and a publicity they do not deserve. If you are a hostage your view is likely to be rather different. And it would be a brave man who declared publicly that such a view was not equally valid.

Some of those who have seen him in action in Libya say they have seen weaknesses alongside his strengths – weaknesses which have been tragically exposed in his latest mission in Beirut, but weaknesses which again stem more often than not from his virtues rather than his failings. They say he is too trusting, far too ready to see the best in people contrary to the evidence. "He frequently mistakes hospitality and good manners for trust", said one. "When the Arabs do decide to trust you (and give you theirs in return) they really establish a firm relationship. But you can't immediately be sure that what is passing for trust is the genuine article. He is too open at times and doesn't see when the Arabs play their classic trick – talking to you in confidence but merely telling you what you want to hear. He doesn't speak Arabic and doesn't have a great insight into Arab thinking and philosophy. Certainly he reads a lot to prepare for a trip, and he asks the press corps pertinent questions and takes in the answers, but his real weakness is his failing to understand some of the characters he's dealing with."

The criticism goes to the heart of what many people feared went wrong in his latest mission to the Lebanon. Where some saw trust others saw gullibility, where some saw openness others saw naïvety and, as one experienced hand made clear, the Lebanon is no place for the inexperienced. But those problems were to be thrown into greater relief much later. In Libya for the moment his personal contacts and evident integrity held the day. He returned to London in February 1985, hailed as a popular hero. And in the minds of the four hostages and their families he was without parallel. "He has done a splendid job", said Robin Plummer as he savoured the first moments of freedom in Tripoli. "He has been a source of strength and support to us in the time we have been seeing him. I cannot find words to say other than, 'thank you'." This simple, heartfelt tribute echoing all the men's feelings was the reward for patience, courage and sympathy. The men all knew their indebtedness to him. No more could be said.

But that was not the end of the commitments he had made in London or in Tripoli. As he does with all those he has helped, he continued to see the four men and their families, to keep in touch by letter or by telephone with them in a way which proved his aim was not to chalk them up as successes on an ecclesiastical score card which would eventually earn him stars. The people as always were at the centre of negotiations – before, during and after the event. He continued, too, as he had promised, to visit the Libyan prisoners in Frankland Jail, County Durham, arranging for their families to visit at convenient times, and honouring the pledges he had made to look after the Libyan prisoners' humanitarian needs. The release of the Britons was not conditional on this "pastoral care" of the Libyans, it was merely part of the same overall mission. These were tributaries of the great humanitarian flow which had its beginning and its end in the fatherhood of God and the brotherhood of men.

LEBANON

A month or so after his disappearance there appeared in the *Spectator* magazine a perceptive cartoon by Garland. It pictured Waite as Gulliver, neat in grey suit, white shirt and tie, tied to the ground by scores of little men grouped in factions round the body of the struggling but helpless captive. Standing on top of his giant frame they dug their heels into his chest or pointed guns at his head. Others looked on from afar, complicit in his captivity if not actively involved in tying down the cords that bound him. It was his predicament in Beirut in a nutshell. "He's a good man who is totally unaware of how bad people can be", said one source. "He's really an innocent with no real perception of the groupings, the factions and the family feuds. He isn't quite wised up to some of the dirty tricks, and doesn't believe how devious and evil people can be." Close friends deny it but do agree that in Beirut the sheer number of people in the operation have complicated his mission to an alarming degree. Trusting one party may have been difficult enough in Iran or Libya – dealing with dozens of separate factions and offshoots of factions is practically impossible. And when these same splinter groups may be fighting it out on the streets, spraying gunfire at random to gain control of one office or apartment block, the danger factor is high.

Trapped by streetfighting in his hotel lobby, with press and radio reporters, as he prepared to leave Beirut one time, he was asked by one journalist what he planned to do next. "Take cover" came his quick reply. But in the long run his humour and adaptability (and even his newly acquired bullet-proof vest) could be relied on to afford him only limited protection in a steadily deteriorating city.

His involvement in Lebanon first became public

knowledge in September 1985, when it was revealed that the American Presbyterian Church had sought his help in the release of one of its ministers, the Rev. Benjamin Weir. The shadowy grouping of Islamic fundamentalists known as Islamic Jihad, controlled to a degree by Iran, had been holding him for over a year. Terry Waite's standing during the Waddell and Coleman mission five years earlier in Tehran had given him a measure of influence among the Iranian authorities and, on the face of it, that influence was being put to good effect.

A second direct appeal came next via the Church from four American hostages held in Beirut. They were Terry Anderson, Thomas Sutherland, Father Lawrence Jenco and David Jacobsen. These (and Weir) were being held in re-taliation for the seventeen Arab guerrillas sentenced in Kuwait for bombing American and French embassies in December of 1983. A mere glance at the timetable of events, and at the interconnecting and mutually dependent bargain that radicals were asking to be struck, illustrates perfectly that the complexity of this latest episode far ex-ceeded anything Terry Waite had so far experienced. None the less, having established some communication with the kidnappers, on 13th November 1985 he set out for the first of his many trips to Lebanese soil. He immediately issued an appeal to press and television crews to leave him room to manoeuvre in his attempts to meet the kidnappers face to face. In typical fashion his presence was designed to have a calming effect on the hostage families. He was there trying to be with them, and that counted for much. "We have a real sign of hope", he announced encouragingly. "I believe there is a real possibility of a breakthrough. I'm optimistic but there is a long way to go." Then he was driven off at speed in the back of a BMW, protected by a group of militiamen. Later he told another group of journalists in the Commodore Hotel (now defunct, but then the base of the international press) that he was nearer meeting the kidnappers but could not disclose their identity for fear of compromising both parties. "A wrong move and people could lose their lives", he said in a repeated request to be left in peace by the newsmen. He intended to go to ground to meet the abductors in person.

His relationship with the press is cordial. He will always have time to talk, and seems pleased to be in their company. In their turn they respect his position, and the two sides co-exist with a rare degree of harmony. "He is high profile wherever he goes," said one Middle East correspondent, "and he likes it. I think also he feels it gives him a degree of protection." He enjoys excellent relations with a number of correspondents there. "He's delightful company and a delightful dinner companion", said one. "On one occasion, one of the periodic internecine battles took place outside our hotel between Amal and the Druse, and for a while we were all trapped. He didn't panic and wasn't afraid. He watched it all, watched us file our stories, and then went to the grill where a few of us were discussing the relative merits of the dishes on the menu while the firing continued."

After his first visit, when he returned empty-handed, he decided to go back to Beirut in mid-December. In the meantime his application for a visa to go to Kuwait to talk over the Islamic Jihad's demands was turned down. After this second visit to the Lebanon he did not return for nearly a year. His to-ing and fro-ing was attracting great attention, and those close to him felt he clearly enjoyed the excitement of it, "not in a nasty, unreasonable way, but just because he is built to enjoy excitement; he thrives on it." Louise Pirouet had seen evidence of that in Uganda, albeit in a more controlled way, on the day of the coup in

Kampala, "I suppose you could say there was a certain *Boy's Own* quality to it then. I mean, he would enjoy driving across Kampala when it wasn't a hundred per cent safe, and slapping the soldiers on the back at checkpoints, wouldn't he? But I'm sure he's matured since then, and in any case the *Boy's Own* element, when it's demonstrated in a responsible adult, can be used to very great advantage. He's courageous – which isn't necessarily to say he's un-afraid. But he's been asked to help hostages and he has a choice: he helps them or he doesn't. He sits back and does nothing. So the excitement, like the *Boy's Own* quality is, in itself, quite neutral." And many people have that precise quality to be grateful for.

When he returned to England between trips he made no effort to play any grand role. He remained a natural if larger than life-sized personality. His work with the YMCA charity and the annual Crisis at Christmas appeal for money for the homeless earthed him to everyday concerns, and though reporters naturally made a bee-line for him he did not attempt to play up to them at all. Sure, he was something of a celebrity but nobody seriously begrudged him that.

There was, however, one slight reservation to which a close friend of long standing admitted. It had occurred rather earlier than the current Beirut episode, but indicated perhaps a tendency to allow his celebrity to run away with him and to lose a sense of proportion as to his own per-sonal fame. It was when he was asked to appear on tele-vision as a chat-show host. The theory was that it should be a serious programme of conversation, with Terry inter-viewing one guest of note per week. The general critical reaction was extremely poor, and few think he emerged with great credit as a result. "We thought at the time," says his friend, "why are you getting involved in that kind of thing? We thought, Terry, that's not you. Television and guest appearances like that aren't for you. The TV isn't about honesty. It isn't where you should be." Perhaps fame had turned his head a little, though on the evidence of his past record it seems equally likely that here was another challenge to be accepted. Another new experience to be tasted. All this was merely a backcloth to Terry Waite's main concern for the hostages.

In the year since he had left Beirut much had been happening – much of it, crucially, out of sight of the world. On 26th July one of the hostages, Father Lawrence Jenco, the Roman Catholic priest, was released, followed in November by another American, David Jacobsen. Terry Waite was there to meet them, and it seemed once again that the envoy's particular touch had paid off.

But events were not that simple. For one thing, in the period between the two release dates Terry Waite made a secret trip to the Middle East and used American helicopters to transport him between Cyprus and the Lebanon. In one sense there was nothing surprising about this, since the hostages were, after all, American. But then on the release of Jacobsen, Terry Waite was seen in the company of Oliver North, the man who is at the centre of the secret American deal to supply arms to Iran. When the Irangate scandal broke it threw a different light on all the previous negotiations, and raised questions which have so far not been conclusively answered. Did Terry Waite know of the secret arms deals? If he did, did he consent to continue as mediator, knowing that his role would be nothing more than a smokescreen? If he did not know, were the Americans using him as an innocent dupe, a useful decoy for the real negotiations which had nothing to do with Christian humility and everything to do with hard bargains and power politics? When David Jacobsen was released he said, movingly, "Terry was a man of hope in our darkest hour. As we sat on the floor in our underwear last Christmas he gave us hope that we would be free men. We love this guy." Nothing which the Americans or the Iranians had done in secret could detract from those words. They would remain true enough. What was in doubt was whether Terry Waite himself had succeeded as a powerless mediator, or whether the Americans had succeeded as hard-boiled negotiators.

Inevitably such speculation tarnished the envoy's image, but he was quick to put the record straight. He knew nothing of the arms deals, he said, did not believe it right to trade weapons for human lives, and said complicity in such a deal would run flatly counter to the job of any humanitarian. When he appeared in Beirut on 12th January he came alone, severing all association with the American dealings which had, he said, jeopardized his mission by driving contacts underground. But still he came, facing what he knew was a perilous mission. He left behind a note saying that if he were to be kidnapped no ransom should be paid and no rescue mounted to save him. He ignored specific advice from the Foreign Office, and, reportedly, from his employer, Dr Robert Runcie, not to go. So why did he do it?

Partly it was to prove the truth of his denial of involvement in any secret deal. Returning to Beirut put distance between himself and the Americans and reaffirmed his independence (never, for him, in question) as a religious representative seeking the release of all hostages. But most significantly it was a hazardous re-affirmation of his promises made to the hostages over a year ago – promises of which he had never lost sight.

Shortly before leaving on this latest journey, he spoke at length to Samuel Van Culin about his reasons for going.

"He said he felt he had to go. He knew he was taking a chance but he had taken chances before. He said he had to fulfil the commitment he had made to them and their families. When you build up a deep and abiding sense of being integrally involved with the pain, the suffering and the hope of individual people, you look at danger with less self-caution."

And other close friends and colleagues say the same. "What he couldn't stand was this intolerable silence", says Gordon Kitney. "When hostages are taken there are seemingly endless weeks of silence when the family is put through immense torture. And I think that's what spurred him on. He can't stand to see people suffer if he can alleviate the pain. Another thing is that he takes the view that when people take hostages they do so out of despair. He utterly condemns the kidnapping, but he realizes that doing so is a way of saying that the world isn't listening to what they are saying. He feels part of his job is to facilitate some sort of communication as a way of improving the chances of peace in the world. He is a man of peace."

But could there also have been another reason behind his decision to return? Could it be possible that the revelation of arms shipments had dealt a powerful blow to honesty and that he, almost by way of atonement, was duty-bound to stake his own personal safety as a surety on goodness in a bad world?

Louise Pirouet, who shared with him the violent times of Amin's Uganda, says what he does is done not out of naïvety. "He knows how bad the world is. Living in Uganda at the time you couldn't be unaware of it. And I certainly remember him talking to me about the difficulty he sometimes had in believing in goodness. If you've trodden on the edges of evil as one did in Uganda at the time, that feeling is not surprising. But he always said that

141

you've got to take the risk of acting openly and honestly with people. However hard it is, you have to try. In the end, he said, you've got to be prepared to give simple goodness a chance."

DATE DUE
